CW00339082

Gran ON THE RUN

(for the money)

Wendy Ellwood

Pixeltweaks
PUBLICATIONS

Published in 2014
© Copyright Wendy Ellwood

ISBN: 978-0-9927514-6-3

Cover and Book interior Design by Russell Holden
www.pixeltweakspublications.com

Pixel✳tweaks
PUBLICATIONS

Acknowledgements

Thanks a million to...

My special mentor, John, who was
behind me all the way in this incredible
journey and yet led me through it

Sister Penny who embraced the cause with
enormous enthusiasm from start to finish,
raising money, listening, advising

Mum, Dad and all the family for taking
on the cause with such vigour

Close friends who sponsored me so generously
and supported and encouraged me in all sorts
of other ways with cakes, prizes and advice

Kath and the Knight Trust for the incredible
boost to our fund raising efforts

Members of Windermere, Kendal and Grange Bridge
Clubs who sponsored me in such huge numbers

Shops/businesses in and around Staveley
who gave raffle prizes and donations

Kendal Lions, Windermere and Ambleside Lions
and Ambleside Rotary for sponsorship

'Staveley chronicler', Justina, for her
amazing photographic input

Westmorland Gazette

For Georgie, Simon, Meg and Heidi

All profits from the book to Diamond Blackfan Anaemia Charity

Contents

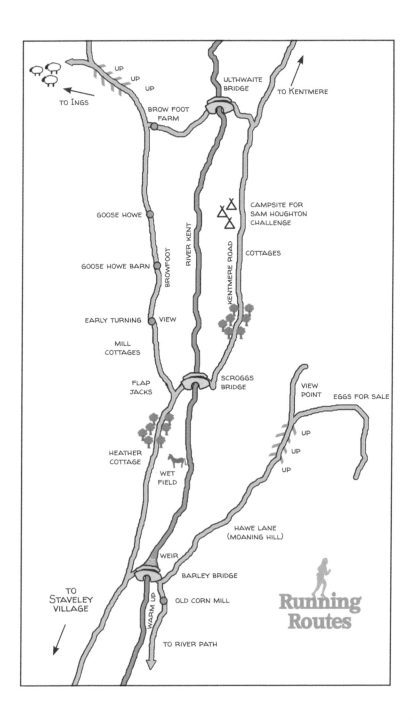

A Resolution

It is a miserable winter's day and I am trying to find out something about Diamond Blackfan Anaemia, which no one seems to have heard of. This is a possible diagnosis for my just two year old granddaughter, Heidi. She has spent 18 months being referred from one health official to another, one hospital to another, one test after another. I am looking for medical information when I click on the DBA charity site and this notice confronts me ...

Final Call for Great North Run 2014

This is a quick update to let you know we only have a couple of places left for the Great North Run 2014, so you need to act now if you want to take part! This year's GNR takes place on the 7th September 2014 over a 13.1 mile course, starting in Newcastle city centre and finishing by the coast in South Shields. Places in the huge fundraising event are very hard to come by so don't let this opportunity slip by, especially such a fantastic chance to raise funds for DBA UK.

Well, what would you do? It is December 2013 when I first see this 'opportunity' of a lifetime! I am looking for answers and here is a challenging question. I start to ask myself if I could do it. Can an unfit pensioner who's never run further than a bus stop before, run for 13 miles. If, very big if, I could achieve it and raise funds to help Heidi's condition in any small way it's a challenge I will relish, an opportunity I won't let slip by.

I have plenty of time to get fit and give it a go. This quest for knowledge is to change the course of my life's focus for the next nine months.

Although it is winter the seed takes hold and begins to grow. I float the idea past husband, John. I think if we both attempt to do it we can get fit and healthy together. He thinks I am mad to consider taking up running at nearly 65 and has no intention of joining me. He has always thought my ability falls far short of my enthusiasm and this is no exception. I don't think he believes my mounting enthusiasm will come to anything. But I've got the idea now and am becoming increasingly consumed by it. And of course he says he'll be right behind me, well, somewhere behind me.

On December 31st 2013 as the clock strikes midnight I close my eyes and make it my new year's resolution to have a go at competing in the Great North Run. Usually I come up with some vague, idealistic resolution, which is neither measurable, timed nor attainable. This is exciting, measurable and timed certainly, achievable, not at all sure. I don't mention my resolution to the friends we are spending new year's eve with as it sounds, and probably is, implausible. I want to see if I can improve my fitness level and sustain my enthusiasm over a month.

So from January 1st I start going out for a daily walk/ jog round the village. My incipient running career is breathless and aimless, but a start, or more of a stop/ start! I am surprised at how little I can run before getting out of breath, just a few hundred yards. I also note how slowly time goes when I try to run. A fifteen minute session with little runs and lots of walking seems to stretch my capabilities. Doubts are creeping in as to whether this seed has got what it takes to grow. The challenge is on: banish the doubts and actually deliver on this resolution.

'Far better is it to dare mighty things, to win glorious triumphs, even though checkered by failure... than to rank with those poor spirits who neither enjoy nor suffer much, because they live in a gray twilight that knows not victory nor defeat.' Theodore Roosevelt.

Warming up in Malta

We head for Malta in the second week of January, to the port of Sliema. I continue with a daily walk/jog before breakfast. Unlike the Lake District the weather is lovely and fresh along the front, with lots of people heading for work or out exercising. I am a bit disheartened when jogging one fine morning, I am overtaken by a lady and her dog, walking! But I must be building up my stamina I vaguely hope. I also note how long a few minutes appears to be in running terms in spite of the fact that the harbour front at Sliema is totally flat. If I didn't intersperse running with brisk walking I'd be back in our hotel room in less than 5 minutes, that's including four storeys in the lift.

In the second week in Malta, with two weeks to go, I decide more positive action is required. I go to the hotel gym and make an appointment with a personal trainer. I'm going to give this project a serious injection of intent, and who better than handsome, fit, young, personal trainer, Mat, to help me. He puts me through my paces then gives me a programme on the running machine and light stretching and upper body building exercises. I try to make it look as though it's all well within my grasp, doing one extra, lifting one heavier, and smiling painfully. I can hardly move for 2 days after that first session of trying to impress Mat, I am so stiff, everything aches. I hope to work with him on a regular basis, but find he is often away, or late in. He doesn't share my enthusiasm for my training. Anyway, the next time I do manage to see him he gets me concentrating on breathing and when pushed says it could be possible for me to have a go at a half marathon sometime in future and I choose to believe him – so onward.

We relax from daily gym sessions in the spa pool and jacuzzi followed by the swimming pool, all very luxurious. Beginning to feel a bit like a budding athlete, I buy some cut-off joggers to try and blend in with all the fit and toned bodies in the gym.

Fitting in doesn't seem to bother John, who buys some canary yellow shorts and matching yellow T-shirt for the gym. I am doing a mixture of mainly walking with two minute jogs thrown in over 25 minutes – two minutes seems a very long time to run continuously and my heart beat goes way over the recommended rate, according to the running machine. Mat advises me to do less running at this stage, keep it to one minute jogs, build up on the walking. It sounds like advice for an old pensioner to me. I get the feeling I'm not a natural born runner!

From a Sitting Start

After three weeks of pleasant Malta sunshine, sightseeing, bridge, good food and a daily work-out we return to cold, gloomy winter in Cumbria.

A month after my new year's resolution I'm not much fitter but my level of commitment is growing. The fact that Heidi has been really poorly while we are away, strengthens my resolve. I check with daughter, Georgie, that she is happy for me to try and run for Heidi on behalf of DBA. She is very encouraging and enthusiastic. She tells me about an NHS programme called *Couch to 5K,* which a few of her friends have tried. This is to transform my fitness campaign.

John downloads the podcasts and the next stage of my plan is underway!

I contact DBA offering to attempt the Great North Run on their behalf, tingling with anticipation, then have an anxious wait for a reply. Finally I hear they will send me a token to register officially. I wait and wait. When I don't hear back from them I am sure they must have realised they don't want someone as old and unfit as me. Finally, nervously, I contact them again only to find the token has gone straight to spam on the computer, so I have to reapply. I am very excited when I finally receive notification and do lots of stretching exercises and dancing around the kitchen.

Dear Wendy Ellwood
Congratulations. You are now registered in the BUPA Great North Run and will be joining 55,999 others on the start line of the world's greatest half marathon on Sept 7th 2014

I'm asked if I want a DBA T-shirt or a vest for the GNR – how REAL is that? At this stage I want what will provide the best cover. Baggy T-shirt and track suit bottoms is how I envisage myself. I now have a unique reference number and entry confirmation, so barring accidents, I will be there. No 'gray twilight' for me!

Just over a month after my resolution, I start *Couch to 5k* programme with enthusiasm and optimism and I resolve to write up each session of my ' jog log', such is my motivation.

Week 1 of NHS programme and the start of my training log. I am told to complete each programme three times before moving on to the next session. This approach suits me as being an indecisive person I enjoy following specific instructions or directions, especially with an end purpose to aim for.

With Laura in my ears I go out for my first 30 minute guided session with a programme and a purpose. It's quite novel and fascinating being told what to do as I go along – a bit like picking up instructions on a treasure hunt. We start with a brisk 5 minute warm-up walk. There is quite a lot of walking with 1 minute jogs thrown in. I'm amazed one minute feels like such a long time when running and I wonder if Laura has forgotten to tell me to stop running. I enjoy the music with its pumping beat and find the half hour goes quickly and painlessly. On my return I have a glass of water and banana as directed by Laura. I don't even like bananas! I dutifully complete week one programme 3 times before progressing to week 2. Having the pod casts on my i pad has revolutionised my approach. I feel focused and motivated, and most importantly, I have a direction. This is SMART goals at their best.

My birthday dawns and the focus is fitness and lycra.

I'm getting seriously geared up now. John buys me a fluorescent yellow belt strap and a very yellow hat as it is so dark and gloomy out there. I also get some proper running pants, very tight and far from flattering.

February 11

On to week 2 with Laura. I am following the same route away from the village each day as it's as flat as it gets round here and it offers a helping of every ingredient needed to produce scenic and tranquil. From our house I cross Barley Bridge and the weir and head away from the village, following the river, along the winding lane which eventually runs out into rough track. There is never much traffic up the lane as it services a few cottages and a couple of farms. I'm up to 90 second runs now, and several of them in the half hour session, though still lots of walking in between, which is suiting me well.

February 13

Are the 90 second runs getting a little easier? I ask myself, on my second outing of week 2. I'm following the same route, out into the country, which tends to be more up on the outward leg, down on the return.

9

A friend suggests that a good challenge along the way could be to take part in a 5k park run when (if) I ever get to running 5k. It should be April according to Laura. Further investigation reveals these park runs take place at 9am every Saturday morning. Penrith is our nearest Parkrun.

FEBRUARY 15

It is my third time on this programme heading UPPPP Browfoot, passing lots of sheep, a handful of old mill cottages and a variety of wildlife and wild flowers, even at this time of the year. I see hundreds of snowdrops on the banks and under trees. These delicate splashes of white bravely appear while we are still in the icy grip of winter. I spot  a rabbit sitting by the wall until I approach, and a deer on the far side of a field. When the distant mountain range comes into view I do a U turn and head for home, following the meandering river back to Barley Bridge where it takes a dive over the weir and plunges under the bridge. There can't be many better road routes than this, even in the rain and low cloud cover, which there is today.

February 17

Monday morning first thing and I'm starting week three with Laura. It's a dull wet day but I'm geared up for it and curious to see what this session involves. I do the usual 5 minute warm up with a couple of three minute jogs in the middle. I just hang on in there as if I was racing for the line after an arduous race, waiting for the three minutes to be up. The first one is harder as its uphill, much easier downhill on the return. 'You've done really well' says Laura with a smile and that makes me feel good.

February 19

I go a bit later today as the weather is overcast at first but brightening later. The sheep are very noisy. The farmer must be due to come and feed them. I am surprised on my return to see a lady lying by the side of the road. A couple of cars have stopped; people are bending down around her. So I decide there's no need for me to stop and, in any case, I strongly suspect Laura will carry on without me! Further down the lane I encounter a flashing ambulance heading towards her. What drama! I don't usually see anyone.

February 21

By the third session of week three's programme I feel I am getting less breathless, less desperate. It will be nice out there when it stops raining. Everywhere is waterlogged, the river is full, fast flowing and noisy. The fields look like boggy marsh land, puddles are turning into lakes, gushing into drains and, according to the long range weather forecast, there is no great expectation that week 4 weather will be any better.

February 23

I awaken to a sea of rain, but decide to go out first thing as the forecast doesn't promise any improvement. I get all my wet weather gear on and off I go, keen to hear what Laura has in stock for me this week. My curiosity is aroused as I move on to the new programme for week four and I am filled with a new helping of enthusiasm. Well, Laura informs me it's two 3 minute and two 5 minute runs with walks in-between. The five minute runs push me to the limit but I feel a grim determination to follow Laura's instructions. The relief when she says 'you can stop running now' is almost tangible. I'm just coping with the rain, avoiding puddles and mini waterfalls gushing out of the banks but I'm getting a bit worried about the two horses in an already waterlogged field and with the river that borders their field still rising. Every hoof print is embedded deep in the muddy swamp. I arrive home dripping, eager for a banana boost and a warm shower.

February 25

What a difference a day makes. It is a beautiful sunny morning. I follow the familiar route, keeping to the roads as the ground is very wet and boggy. It won't be long before the daffodils are out, second only to snowdrops in their determination to cheer us through the gloomy months. The water in the river is sparkling today and when I get to the usual turning point I'm rewarded with beautiful clear mountain views – so much more enjoyable than yesterday and I am sure I am quicker on the way back, especially in last five minute run. I have now worked out if I turn sooner it's because I'm covering the ground faster – good job it's not quick thinking I'm in training for.

February 27

After non-stop rain again yesterday we are rewarded with another beautiful morning, cold though, when I get out. I do my usual 5 minute warm up walk and say hello to one of the sad looking horses planted in the water-logged field. I break into a jog when instructed, then am surprised when Laura tells me to stop running when I am still fit to go. I realise I have gone back to week 3 pod cast by mistake and that has no five minute

runs. I try to switch to week 4 but I can only start at the beginning. I'm not very good with this technology, it's so frustrating having to stop and fiddle around with it. I turn at the high point as usual but today the tops are iced and shimmer in the watery sun

light. Anyway, not wanting to short change Laura, I do an extra circuit round the village and along river path on my return. I must remember I'm on to week 5 next time out.

FEBRUARY 28

I get up bright and early, thinking it will be ok to run two consecutive days as we're off to York at 10am for a weekend of bridge and I'm not sure how easy it will

be to fit jog sessions in over the next few days of bridge and more bridge. Anyway it is a lovely white, bright morning, so I wrap up as warm as I can, layer upon layer, hat, gloves, topped off by my fluorescent belt strap. Laura's encouraging voice welcomes me to week 5 and off we go, out in to the cold morning air, breath puffing out in clouds, for our brisk warm up to pumping music. We get as far as Barley Bridge (50m) when I slip and realising there is ice all around me, I capitulate without a fight. So here I am back home and actually a bit disappointed.

MARCH 1

Saturday morning dawns crisp and bright in York. John and I go and find the Museum Park in centre of York.

We buy a paper and find a bench in the sun for John to sit and read, like a pensioner, while I embark on the first of week five's programme, three five minute jogs, interspersed with walking, around and around the park, along the river and back. John doesn't even look up when I pass; such encouragement is quite underwhelming. Then it's off to reward myself with eggy bread brunch in a quaint little café overlooking York Minster.

March 3

We're back home for lunch, so it's off up Browfoot for two ten minute sprees in the afternoon. Longest run yet, ten whole continuous minutes, twice, and all I can think is I'll never, ever run for anything approaching an hour when 10 minutes is such a feat.

March 5

In Faversham, Kent for this one. I came down on the train yesterday to visit daughter, Georgie, husband Simon, Meg and Heidi.

I wait for a time when Meg is at school and Heidi is having a sleep. They live opposite a recreation ground with various paths around its perimeters; so basically I just go round and round. Even though it's the last of week five's programmes, I am a bit shocked when Laura tells me to jog for twenty whole minutes without stopping, but I do it, slowly, painstakingly, but I do it. I even inject a tiny bit of pace when she says one minute to go. I finish with an extra speedy run up to the sandwich shop, talk about motive, where I buy some sandwiches and a cake to celebrate my feat with daughter. It's easy to keep fit when I'm down here as they have an old house on four floors and two little ones who keep one permanently on one's feet.

MARCH 8

On to week 6 but I can't get out before late-ish afternoon, what with phone calls, visitors and the village jumble sale, which I can't bear to miss – all those bargain books and toys. John bought me a proper running kit in a pack while I was away, lycra hat, gloves and a bright pink rain coat. So exciting, my latest fashion accessories! It is a nice day but I'm keen to wear my new gloves and hat. Not a bad session as I am expecting another 20 minute run, but it is broken into two tens. John and I cover my regular route in the car later to ascertain the distance. It's 2.2 miles, so that's six times further I've got to run in just six months ... surely that can't be possible!

March 10

A real feel of spring in the air inspires me to make an early start on the second edition of week six, in spite of a sore throat and cold. Eating a brazil nut, whilst having a cold and running, is not a good start. I have a fit of coughing just after Barley Bridge and have to return home for water and a throat sweet. I then go on to complete my session with Laura without further ado. I pass someone running the other way up Browfoot who calls out to ask if I am on Couch to 5k programme – not sure what made her ask that, I was beginning to think I looked like a regular runner (albeit a slow one)!

March 12

Another beautiful day for the last of my week six runs but I don't feel like running as my cold doesn't seem to be going. Anyway I won't take no for an answer so I go and it actually makes me feel better. Today is the first day I haven't worn a hat, gloves still, but no hat. I cheat slightly as I do a lap of the village, taking me along the river path, through the wood yard, smelling of freshly baked bread and back up Main Street, already busy, before heading up Browfoot. This means I can turn before I get to the steep bit. As I finish Laura says I can now consider myself an official runner as I've just done 25 minutes non-stop. I do like Laura even though she makes me eat bananas.
Me, an official runner!

March 14

I must be mad. As I get to Barley Bridge Laura says why not vary the route or the routine as we enter week seven. So I take one step back from the bridge and head UP Hawe Lane and up and up. I start with the

compulsory brisk walk for five minutes, upwards, and when it is almost vertical I commence 25 minutes running ... upwards. It feels like I am jogging on the spot but step by step I edge closer to the top.

This is a regular walk of ours to get the eggs, an hour circuit. The up part we call Moaning

Hill. Friends and family are allowed to give vent to all their moans, but once we get to the top they (moans, not friends and family) should all blow away into the clouds – in any case, I don't want to hear any more after that. Grandson, Nathan always makes particularly good use of Moaning Hill on his visits! Once at the top it's a fairly level stretch across open fell side, before a steepish descent. No eggs I note as I pass the box. I finish the allocated run time way before home so do quite a bit extra – but I'll be back on my regular route tomorrow for sure!

March 16

Back on the old track and off before breakfast. I need

to run off last night's Chinese meal. It all seems a bit easier after Friday's sheer mountain climb; suddenly Browfoot doesn't seem quite so uppish and I positively enjoy the downward home run. Twenty-five minutes of continuous running would have seemed impossible a month ago – proof of progress.

MARCH 18

I intend to go early this morning as John is off inspecting schools before 7am but it is bucketing down so I postpone my outing. However the rain is relentless so I have no option but to get all the wet weather gear on and head out, intrepidly. Meanwhile Georgie and Simon have taken Heidi up to Great Ormond Street today while I'm out there enjoying the fresh country air. I think of them as I jog along in the rain to round off week seven. I arrive home, water dripping from my hat and my hair, cold drops onto my face but a certain satisfaction that I've been out on such an uninviting day and achieved Laura's target.

March 20

It's a cold, windy day. I find a large cover all fleece of John's to wear, because I'm conscious of my skin tight running pants. I set out on week eight's adventure which involves running for 28 minutes. It is on my way back along Browfoot that I encounter a little white car – unusual to see cars along this stretch of lane. Out jumps the driver and starts taking photos of me, it's John. Needless to say while he has left the car blocking the lane in pursuit of a good photo opportunity another car appears – a veritable traffic jam! John takes a few more photos along the route – how glad am I that I've worn his big fleece. A bit of a panic when I get back, no bananas, just a giant warm croissant, what am I to do but eat it!

March 22

Would you believe I bought some more lycra stuff yesterday – a fluorescent pink, long (cover bum) top and a fluorescent yellow drinks rucksack/belt. I set off this morning in several layers, with new pink on top, on a crisp, bright morning. I don't realise how crisp it is until I see Kentmere Horseshoe is covered in a white veil. There is also light, sparkling snow on the verges, sprinkled

 like pearls all around the now flowering, defiant daffodils. I pass my usual turning spot and run on as far as Goose Howe barn, where I turn, creating a Browfoot record.

March 24

It's the last of week eight's 28 minute runs this morning and a beautiful chilly morning it is. The cars are all frosty white as I set off, and baby lambs are huddling together in the fields all around. What

a cold night they must have had, poor little things. Only the far distant mountains are wearing white hats today. As I run back along the river I can hardly see with the sun reflecting off the choppy water. I'm toasty warm by the time I get home in spite of the frosty temperature.

March 26

I start my run full of anticipation. It's the first of the last three of *Couch to 5k*, week nine, so I know it will be my first full 30 minute run. I've found an old pedometer and tried to set it on distance. So how close will my 30 minute jog come to covering 5k. I go slightly further up Browfoot, beyond Goose Howe Barn, and turn at Goose Howe. Another new record I note, they're falling fast and furious now. No snow on any tops this morning, just beautiful autumnal oranges and greens, bathed in sunlight. On my return I am snapped by John from our bedroom window (lacking the enthusiasm of jumping in the

car for action shots). Once at our front door I am anxious to check the pedometer. I must admit to being a bit disappointed as it shows 2.8 miles in 30 minutes and 5k is just over 3 miles. So my next challenge is to up the distance in the time.

March 28

A dull, drizzly morning and a cold wind await me when I leave the warmth of home. I get just over the bridge when a biting wind bites me and I run home for another layer. Well, it is all about the pedometer this morning. Me against the clock! I don't count the 5 minute warm-up or warm-down, just the pure run. I really try to up the pace when I turn for home, so am disappointed to see I have covered 2.3 miles in 30 minutes. I just sort of assumed that Laura would get me running 3 miles in 30 minutes, I feel a little bit let down in her. On Sunday I have to run 5k as I become a graduate of *Couch to 5K* but I know I won't do it in 30 minutes. Keep on running .

March 30

I thought I'd set off early this morning for the last of *Couch to 5k* while it is nice and quiet. The clocks spring forward today, so 7.10am is actually 8.10am – still quite early for a Sunday morning. Well, I open the front door and 200 cyclists speed by, closely followed by another 100. Le tour de Staveley is on. I have to be careful not to get run over. I am on a mission to run over three miles in whatever time it takes. I find a stop watch so I can measure time over 30 minutes more accurately than using my watch and I have a pedometer ready and willing. I do my 5 minute warm up walk before starting all my electronic devices. I feel weighed down with them. Then off I run on the usual route. I'm very conscious after turning for home of covering ground, keep checking pedometer, which seems to be on a bit of a go slow. I am well past our house when the lovely Laura congratulates me for 30 minutes running, but three miles isn't up, so on I run, and on, along the river path, check , through the village, check, back over the bridge, past our house (for 3rd time) check – wow, it's finally passed the 3 mile – stop, check timer - 15 min 20 it must be joking, I know I'm over half an hour; so after all that, the timer doesn't work and I don't know my time. But at least I now have 3 miles under my belt. I stagger home – no 5 minute warm down for me today. I am now a graduate of *Couch to 5k* and I celebrate the three whole miles by collapsing into a chair with glass of water and a banana booster. I'm up off the couch and running.

The Reluctant Runner

April 1

Well I haven't given up on Laura but she just offers three podcasts for 5k+, speed, stamina and something else. I shall mix and match them, doing each one 3 times, starting with Speed. It's warm and sunny by the time I set out around midday. It takes me almost half a day to get ready as I keep adding to my repertoire. I fill my new water container, set the new, working stop watch/timer, find Laura waiting on the i player, plug in the ears, set the pedometer, attach the running rucksack ... worn out, ready for running. But first I complete a five minute warm up walk, with lots of instructions about how to go faster. As soon as Laura says 'run' I fire everything up and I'm off, rattling over the bridge. And there is John, walked all that way from the front door to catch

a glimpse of me through the camera lens.

I'm finding it hard today, my legs feel a bit heavy, my mouth is dry. I reach for my new water container but no water comes out, push it up, pull it down, half turn, nothing, and trying to run up a hill at the same time. I will not allow myself to stop but I have to have some water by now so I take the main top off and manage to get a small amount in my mouth and a large amount down my neck, and it's cold. Rehydrated with half a mouthful of water, I push on as fast as I can, finally completing the full 35 minutes. I'd love to say how far I have run in the time. I checked the moment I stopped – 00.00 was my distance reading!!! I'd only forgotten to start it. I'm mindful to go out all on my own next time – no Laura, ear phones, hat, gloves, pedometer, timer, water, running rucksack, none of them.

I'm off to see my parents tomorrow so may have to miss a day as I don't get back until late on Thursday. Perhaps by then I will have resolved my issues with Laura and the entourage of gimmicky gadgets.

April 6

It's been a few days too long since I last exercised. Unfortunately I took to my bed ill on Friday, worse on Saturday, better by Sunday. The forecast is for rain all day and it is torrential, but it is important I get back into

my running routine. So off I go, reluctantly, out into the wet, grey morning, having eaten very little since Thursday lunchtime. No pedometer or timer today, keep it simple. I push myself on thinking, I'll turn here, on, turn, no, and so up Browfoot where just short of my usual turning place I capitulate and head for home. Lots of puddles, high roaring river, splashy cars, dripping glasses, squelchy shoes – what a relief to get home to a boost of potassium and a steamy, hot shower. Just a 30 minute run ticked off, slow and wet.

April 8

Oh dear, a bit of a poor effort again today! I haven't eaten much for a few days now because of sickness/ tummy bug recurring, so lacking in even more energy and enthusiasm. Training programme for *The Great North Run*, which is not one I'm following, sets 20 minutes easy for today. I'll take that in preference to Laura's 35 minutes. It's just about all I can manage in my present state of lethargy, a bit of a circuit round the village, which is a shame because it's quite a nice day after two days of non-stop torrential rain. In fact there is nothing easy about this 20 minutes clock watching.

April 10

I'm back! Woke up wanting to go this morning – out of bed and away with just Laura, the pedometer, sunshine and a feeling of well-being. Three miles is my aim, a record breaking repeat. Although there is still a fair amount of surface water, the rivulets, pouring from craggy banks all along the way, have slowed to a trickle; the daffodils are drooping, weary from their winter watch, but the trees have the promise of green. The lambs look sleepy, absorbing the early sun. I run past Goose Howe Barn, and just beyond Goose Howe, my furthest point yet and another record for the collection, but as the  lane falls away before me I can't face the prospect of running downhill only to have to turn and run back up. So I do a quick swivel, taking in my last glimpse of Kentmere Horseshoe shimmering in light. A fairly easy run back follows, 3.1 miles, and in about 40 minutes. Water, banana, shower – normal service resumed.

April 11

A beautiful sunny morning it may be but it's not a running day. However, when the Staveley Chronicler, offers to come with me and take some photos of my running route, it's too good an opportunity to miss. The Staveley Chronicler is in fact a title I have bestowed on local photographer, Justina, who has a record of everything and everybody that moves in or around the village. Nothing escapes her quizzical lens. So I know these will be images to cherish, showing my usual route off at its very best. I don the luminous lycra and we set off ... walking, snapping. As we veer off up Brow Foot there is a sign

on one of the cottages ' *flapjacks - donations for homes in Mexico*'. We oblige, taking two huge flapjacks. Justina spots a woodpecker in the distance, and there he is zoomed in a picture. There are lambs aplenty to watch as we stroll on past Goose Howe. I even run down the uncharted hill and back just for the camera. Not quite as steep as I'd imagined – I determine to add that on to my next run. In the wink of an eye we're back; the pedometer reads 3.2 miles. Walking is just so easy! And then there are Mexican flapjacks to eat. No running banana today.

April 12

Saturday morning, I need to get running as we've got visitors due. I miss the certainty of my programme: which Laura podcast should I go with, should I just go by time, distance, or The Great North Run training programme? Reluctantly, as I'm going through the door I select Speed which I've done once before, shut the door and I've forgotten the pedometer. Thirty-five minutes running at pace with the music. Laura's saying 1,2,3,4 ever faster, and I'm saying but I'm going up hill! I go well on down the lane before I turn and even manage some intermittent bursts of speed on the way back. I'm feeling good today, pleased with the increased speed, until a lone runner flies past me without a nod or a word, over the bridge and out of sight. It's generally chilly and overcast, starting to rain as I get back – glad we took the pictures yesterday.

April 14

Monday morning. Waking up to the sun coming through the curtains gets me quickly up and off. I have just one Saturday in April when I can attempt to take on one of my challenges from back in February, a Park Run race and that's at the end of this week, Easter Saturday. But before I register I want to know that I can complete 3 miles in less than 40 minutes. My research suggests that's about the slowest time people run it in. I don't mind being last but I don't want them all waiting to for me to finish before they can go home. So it's a pedometer and stopwatch run. I time myself at 21 minutes for the first half, then turn. The return is easier, downhill . As I approach home I have one eye on pedometer and one on the stopwatch. As mileage hits 3, I press the stop button at 38.32 min. So ... ready or not ... Penrith Parkrun here we come!

The Race is on!

I'm in serious training mode. This morning's aim is to cover 3 miles in reasonable time. As I turn up towards Browfoot I am confronted by a big red ACCESS ONLY sign, then a van, a works lorry and trailer and a tractor. They are tarmacking bits of the road, upsetting the usual tranquillity. It is with difficulty I pass them as they take up the entire width of the lane, filling it with the smell of tarmac. Anyway, squeeze past them I do and run on to my furthest point yet, well beyond Goose Howe before turning for home and renegotiating the traffic jam. It's a new record again, though not a big one in terms of distance. I will make it to the end of the lane one day, undulating though it is. I complete the run without taking a time today, just building up to Saturday. I must register for the Parkrun before I chicken out. I need to download a bar code to enter.

APRIL 18

With the focus firmly fixed on tomorrow's Parkrun I decide to run through the village and up the main road to Ings as there is a good footpath and, more to the point, I perceive it as flat. Of course as soon as I start running all the hills pop up and it proves quite a haul up out of the village. I spy the Staveley chronicler out

30

on bike with camera heading in the opposite direction. It's Good Friday; the sun is shining and loads of cars are heading for the Lakes – what a noisy vrooming road! Along the path I am overtaken by the bike and camera, so this run will be recorded but it's nowhere near as picturesque as my usual route. I am almost blinded by the sun on the return run, but where there are shadows on the pavement they are dappled by the fast emerging leaves. In and out of sun and shade, heading towards me and then away, risking life and limb to cross the busy main road and back, the Staveley chronicler pops up with a camera and pops off again. As I reach home and clock up 3.1 in 39.28mins, just within my limits for Parkrun time, I reflect that the flat road doesn't feel any easier; I'm happier in the real countryside. What will Penrith be like, I wonder. I have to eat pasta tonight, something to do with carb loading.

April 19

Penrith Parkrun day dawns bright and clear. After an early banana on the move we're off up the motorway at break-neck speed having set off later than intended. With pressure mounting, cars, traffic lights, islands, we follow the sat nav along a busy dual carriageway and see a whole herd of runners gathered on the far side of a field with no apparent approach road. With about 9 minutes to the start of the race I think it's all over and I'm not sure whether I feel relief or disappointment, but John manages a u turn, back to the island and heads for the field. I jump out of the car and run towards the pavilion to register. I am told to join the starting line-up and have my barcode with me at the finish. And we are off. No time for a warm up, no time for a race plan, no time for a panic. There I am at the back with everyone else in front of me.

 I am slightly shell shocked at the early speed; in no time at all the majority of the field is way out in front of me. I have to remind myself it isn't actually a race in spite of the fact they all seem intent on getting to the front. We've driven all the way up, I can't just drop out, fade from the back, which is my overriding inclination, no alternative but to keep going, puffing and panting. The route is two circuits round the edge of a running field, plus through a wood and round a sports pavilion, part track, part uneven grass but level. I am encouraged towards the end of the first circuit when I overtake a couple who've broken into a walk. The only problem is everyone else is so far ahead I don't have anyone to follow but at least there are two runners just behind me.

I will never be able to run 13.1 miles I tell myself frequently, more to the point, can I even finish 3, I wonder as I reluctantly embark on the second lap, just a headful of negative thoughts. Finally I enter the home straight, no cheering crowds, no frantic race for the finish, just a young lad surging past me, but to my great relief I reach the finish line and get my bar code scanned and what's more there are a few walkers behind me. Negative thoughts are quickly forgotten once the task is complete – a bit like child birth. Though I have a far more challenging delivery to come!

This e mail awaits me on my return:

enrith parkrun results for event #11. Your time was 00:35:50
ongratulations on completing your 1st parkrun and your first at Penrith today. You nished in 77th place and were the 29th female out of a field of 83 parkrunners nd you came 1st in your age category VW65-69. Well done on your first run.

I am pleased with the time and ecstatic with 1st in my age category. Closer examination shows I am the only one in my age category! None the less – mission accomplished. I'm not sure I could carry on with all this antenatal pain if it wasn't for the promised euphoric aftermath.

Stepping Stones through Spring

April 21

Easter Monday. I leave everyone in bed. Nathan, teenage grandson, was thinking of joining me but all is quiet and he doesn't appear from his bed. My aim this morning is to cover 3 miles in a reasonable time, calm and steady. It's a nice day, just a bit breezy, lot of noisy crows around. I am pleased to be all on my own today after Saturday's Parkrun trauma. I don't even take Laura which is probably why I notice the birds singing. It isn't the same with Laura since the nine week programme finished. I'm thinking of going it alone.

April 23

I leave them all in bed again as I need to keep moving. Just going for a perfunctory run, usual route, get it over with. Well on up the lane I am enchanted to notice

the grass banks on either side of the lane are hailing a new season, an injection of colour - a few early bluebells, dandelions, wild primroses and splashes of white along the banks. The fresh air is warmer and the green is greener. Although I miss Laura telling me what to do and when to do it, it feels liberating to be able to hear natural sounds, birds singing, water gushing, lambs, silence.

April 24

I set off around lunchtime today. I'm doing consecutive days as we're off to Jersey early tomorrow morning and I doubt I'll fit a run in when we arrive. I decide to go off road today as we've had some good weather lately and I don't think it will be too muddy. I've promised myself this all winter. I wear my all terrain trainers with my new marathon socks; I couldn't find any half marathon socks so I settled for these high quality accessories – there is a specified one for each foot – L and R. Somehow they must help me go further – I'll believe anything, try anything!

The chosen route takes me along the river path, past the magical bluebell woods which fill the air above them with shades of blue. It is invigorating running across the open meadows which follow on such a lovely day. It makes me want to sing something from the Sound of Music, whilst frolicking like a lamb. I resist on both counts. Over a stile, and all too soon I'm back

on the lane and it's a steep one, which heads up and up as it twists and turns to a high point, looking down on Staveley in a single glance, before a steady descent to our house. It's Jersey's Festival of Bridge for the next ten days. I hope I find some good running routes.

April 27

I missed yesterday's run for lots of good excuses, so I have to fit one in today. I set out from St Aubins Bay running along the sea wall path. It is actually flat all the way with clear views to St Helier and the castle. It is a very blustery day, but the path is busy with families, dogs, runners and bikes all out enjoying a bit of exercise. This coastal path offers such a different experience for the runners from my usual winding country lanes. Using my watch, I turn at about 17/18 minutes and jog back straight into a head wind to meet at the car. 36 minutes run, no idea of the distance, but a lively and exhilarating experience.

Following a large lunch and an authentic Jersey ice cream, I am ejected from the car at the start of St Helier's fitness trail.

The plan is for me to run right around St Brelades Bay to St Aubins Bay. The tide is right out, leaving wide sandy beaches exposed. I get stitch after 5 minutes, which must be due to the Jersey ice cream but I keep running slowly, painfully through it. Next I get a totally dry mouth, then another slight attack of stitch. After about 15 minutes of crisis running I settle into the run and begin to enjoy my stunning, level seaside surroundings. However, it feels like a long way winding round the bays, with my destination a mere pinprick on the horizon. Finally I wind it in, as the cars and houses loom larger. I arrive at my destination in about 45 minutes.

May 1

I decide I'd better fit in a 30 minute jog round the lanes. Unfortunately I get a bit lost and land up on the main road with a steep, pathless incline back to Acacia Cottage, our erstwhile home. Cars and nettles threaten me all the way back.

May 3

Saturday bridge competition is all afternoon and evening, so I have to fit in a run between breakfast and lunch. I had suspected it might be quite difficult scheduling runs in around bridge sessions but scheduling around eating is proving to be the main problem! Anyway I opt for a local lane run again, determined not to get lost and land up on the main road. But of course that is exactly what I do, and the noise and volume of the traffic is horrendous as it is a bank holiday. I don't greatly enjoy running round busy, narrow, pathless lanes in Jersey.

May 5

Sadly the last day of our holiday dawns and my last Jersey run. I plot my course on the beach. The sand near the harbour wall is too soft, the sand near the sea is too wet but the sand in between , like baby bear's porridge is just right, firm yet with some give. Actually it's great running on that surface with the sea lapping up close by, a real sense of freedom, like I'm the romantic heroine on a film set. In the words of Spencer Davis, I just want to 'Keep on running.' Mind you I probably feel like that because I know I can't, we're going to be timed out. So it is goodbye to Jersey and the end of the first 4 months of my new year's resolution.

Move on up

I arrive back from Jersey ready to embark on the final 4 months. I have reached the half-way point. I set my aims for the next two months: I need to move on up to 8 miles of continuous running and to put myself through another Parkrun for character building and race training.

May 6

It's good to be back on the old favourite route. As I approach Browfoot the sun comes out and highlights all the new growth – yellow, white, blue and green, colours all along the banks, in the trees, in the gardens, pinks, purples – what a difference two weeks makes. Being back on such beautiful, familiar territory and with so much support behind me I feel energised. It's not till I get back, check the pedometer that I note it reads 4.1 miles. Result! I only have to multiply by just over three now- that's all!

May 8

Well! If I felt buoyed up by generous sponsors on Tuesday, how elevated do I feel today after hearing DBA is to receive £5000 from The Knight Trust. Now I know I can do it – I have to move on up, there's no backing out in the face of such generosity, such support. It's a grey and murky morning as I set off but once out there the colours are still vibrant and rain drops glisten on blades of grass all along the banks. Kentmere Horseshoe is shrouded in clouds but it has a dreamlike quality in its calm, shadowy presence. I'm going for the 4 miles again today and am really enjoying being out there.

I complete the run in about 50 minutes but I'm not timing today, as my focus is on going further – I'm still a long, long way off 13.1 miles and half way into the project. I should be up to just over 6.5 miles by now; that's many a mile to add on.

May 11

Oh dear! I may have felt good on 8th but took to bed for next 2 days with migraine. We were supposed to be in Worcester for the weekend but John had to go alone. Meanwhile, back at the ranch I managed to eat an omelette last night so am roughly on course this morning and think I should give it a go. I don't want to get behind at this stage.  It is a typical sunshine and showers day as I set off. My aim is not ambitious – it is to run round the village as far as my energy will take me, no great expectations. I am pleased on return that pedometer shows 2.8 miles, so of course I have to carry on down the lane and back to get it to 3 miles. I wouldn't want to know the speed – it is slow. Eating my banana I feel quite good about myself doing that. In fact I always feel good when I've been out. It's the getting myself out that I struggle with.

Back to normal today as I set off for an early morning run with just the pedometer and new 'shot bloks'. I went into a running shop yesterday, what an industry! I wished I could afford women's X Bionic marathon capris at £80 but in the event I just bought 'Shot Bloks' energy chews, and portable power Sport Beans (to be tried next time).

My aim today is to extend the 3 mile Browfoot route. Once out there I have a sudden change of plan and decide to veer off up the Crook Road for a change. The reason I have not tried this route before is that it is quite a well-used cut through route from Staveley to Windermere and there is no pavement. However as it's only 7am I decide it's worth giving it a go. The road is winding and lightly undulating but has beautiful open views, both near and distant to the left. Half way along I sample one of my new shot bloks. My dubious hope is that together with my marathon socks they will add a bit of distance and speed. As for distance it's not a round route so I have the usual - to turn or not to turn that is the argument. The more I run on, the further it

is to run back but the nearer I get to my goal. After a bit of a fight I give in and turn. Coming back down the Crook Road there are great views of Staveley, a village firmly nestling in a valley. A couple of houses are being built on the edge of the village and workmen are just getting started, banging and clattering, lorries arriving and unloading, waking the village up. A couple are out walking their dogs. A man is heading back with a paper. Approaching the village from this direction presents it through a wider angle lens. I am disappointed when on return home I have only run 4.3 miles because it feels like it should have been a lot more. Not confident that the beans will improve performance greatly, I'm going to have to look for magic trainers!

May 15

I'm seriously missing Laura. Without her I'm simply making the plan up as I go along. It often takes me by surprise. Routinely I find myself jogging round the village, up Browfoot. On a bit of a drizzly day, I'll do just that, 3 miles. Today I keep going beyond Goose Howe and down to the tree and the wall, my furthest point, and turn – NO - administer a portable power bean and keep going. Now, full of beans, well one, I want to go further, I need to go further. So I push on until I reach Browfoot Farm. That's an impressive barrier broken, the furthest I've run up this valley. Elated I turn and head back, mostly downhill from this point. 4.2 miles says the pedometer when I reach home. I could have sworn it was nearer 5 miles. So sure am I that pedometer is wrong, I get John to take me up in the car to measure the distance. Driving on to the top of Browfoot I discover there is a lot further to run to reach the top of valley, and very up and down it is too, much more up than down on the outward leg. I also discover, don't like to admit it, that the pedometer appears to work!

May 17

On a beautiful sunny morning there's no lying in bed; it's straight up Browfoot. I enjoy crystal clear views as far as the eye can see and flowers on the banks, especially bluebells. Trees are beginning to provide shade up parts of the lane as they form a dappled green archway overhead and dappled black shadows on the pavement. A three mile round run is all I have time for as we're off to Hawes for the day to meet a friend. She has come to Yorkshire as husband is doing the Three Peaks Challenge for charity, over Pen-y-ghent, Whernside and Ingleborough. The participants cover 24.5 miles in around 12 hours. We see clusters of hot, weary walkers at a drinks station near Ribblehead Viaduct as we make our scenic way through the Dales. The prospect of walking 24.5 miles in hot sunshine is horrific

beyond my imagination, but then so is running 13.1 miles in whatever the weather. For today I banish those thoughts and we enjoy sitting chatting over several coffees in a hotel garden overlooking Wensleydale bathed in yellow sun while the walkers traverse the peaks and suffer in scorching sun.

May 19

A pre-breakfast 3 mile run before setting off for Kent on the train is what I settle for today. There's lots of exercise in Faversham but no time for runs. Ten minutes after arrival we're out with the scooters and the grandchildren in the park. Georgie heads off to the shops leaving me in charge. Crisis as Meg goes flying off her scooter, over the handle bars and lies in a still heap, screaming and screaming. I can only reach her slowly as I have to scoot Heidi along as fast as I dare. I nervously ascertain that nothing is broken and watch helplessly as blood from Meg's knee drips into her white sock. The three of us and two scooters limp to a park bench to await rescue. Not a promising debut!

A trip to Butterflies nursery with Heidi is quite delightful as she skips and runs along, holding hands – holding hands reassures me she's not going to fall at any moment. She has slightly pink cheeks and energy; energy to run round and round the hall with a doll in a buggy and me in hot pursuit. We both enjoy our morning out. Safely home it's up and down the stairs, in and out of the garden – I don't need to run when I'm in Faversham to keep fit!

Coming home on the train I am discomfited to read an article by *Fiona MacRae* headed:

Too much exercise harms your heart. She states that 'as we get older ... training for a marathon ... could cause us to collapse or finding ourselves needing an electronic pacemaker'. They know this because they 'put mice through their paces on an uphill treadmill'.

And here's me been thinking all this exercise, hard though it is, must be doing me good!

MAY 23

Back in Cumbria and it's a cold, damp and very windy morning, not exactly inviting but then I think 3 miles up the lane and back is the easy option, the hard one's in Kent! A perfunctory run ticks today off, but I'm mindful of the need to up the distance, break another barrier.

MAY 25

A brighter, more inviting morning. I'm aiming for around 4 miles. No podcasts, pedometers or timers just a couple of jelly beans to help me up the hills. Heading towards Scroggs Bridge I hear a cuckoo calling, first one of the year. Then it seems to echo into the distance, further and further away til I can hear it no more. For a while I am transported into my daydreams, and forget about turning. I'm usually waiting to turn, watching the watch or pedometer, arguing with myself, pushing myself on to the next farm, barn, tree. It's just amazing for me to forget about turning. When I finally do turn I have quite a good run back, conscious of using all Laura's tips – shoulders down and relaxed, heel to ground first, small steps. She may not be running with me but she is not forgotten. Banana, shower and I'm good as new. Well, my heart's still beating on its own!

May 27

A bit of excitement today – I run my furthest yet up Browfoot. Sad though it may sound this is my world at the moment, thrills, aspirations, hopes, fears, all centre around a new year's resolution. I think it's time I finally get to the end of the lane. I pass the farm and head into un-run country, up the winding lane, round the bend and up some more, another bend and up some more. I encounter rugged open countryside, lambs, fields set against backdrop of distant fells – well, you'd expect panoramic views when you get this high! As I round yet another bend, another relentless climb before me, I know I am not going to make it to the final frontier today, I simply do not have enough breath. The mouse on a treadmill comes to mind! So I turn and enjoy a long downward run. At the farm I divert my route off to the left, through the middle of the farm yard and along the stony path connecting the lanes on either side of Kentmere Valley. While the uneven path makes for hard running, boggy at times, it's scenic viewing, running parallel to a babbling brook. It leads through a gate, over picturesque Ulthwaite Bridge and right onto Kentmere road. And so I jog towards home on this new circular route, which is gently downhill all the way from here. Circular routes are the best way forward for me, or should I say round, as I don't have the constant bickering about when and where to turn. The euphoria comes when I reach home, check the pedometer, and see 5.01 miles. Just over times 2.5 now, it's coming down, though I can't actually imagine myself being able to double that 5 miles. It stands as such a monumental achievement to date.

May 28

Following on from the excitement of the last outing, I decide on a time trial this morning. It's cold and wet again. How far can I run in 30 minutes, that is my burning question. I am disappointed when I clock 30 minutes and pedometer records 2.40 miles. Which one isn't working properly, is my immediate thought. But I've tried that excuse before. I need to find another gear, or perhaps a reconditioned engine, better still upgrade the old vehicle!

Time is Running

MAY 30

I can't believe it's the end of May. Time is moving swiftly on but the running isn't. I decide to start with a quick tour round the village as I want to see what is happening with the big Staveley Trails run today. I wondered about trying to join them but it's mostly off road and highly challenging. Where I see Hawe Lane as akin to climbing Everest, for them it's just an easy slope.

The runners are gathering. There are tents in the park, a bouncy castle, a loud speaker is warming up, yellow arrows and signs have appeared, a temporary car park has opened in the old cricket field – and they're charging £1. They could have mowed it first, the grass is waist high! Anyway, I leave the buzz of atmosphere behind as I repeat the circuit run of a couple of days ago. Coming down the Kentmere side, I count twelve cars, two vans, a motorbike, a tractor and three bikes, approximately, I may have missed a car or two – talk about rush hour. I think a lot of it could be to do with the trail races which are going up that way later. With another 5 mile run completed I walk down to the park to see the fell runners coming back along the river from their 10k off road circuit and later the 17k runners staggering to the finish line. I feel a spontaneous urge to applaud them as they pass. They look exhausted and so they must be - respect! What will I feel like, look like, if ever I run 13.1 miles? My head is consumed by such thoughts, doubts.

June 2

I set out with heavy legs and an unenthusiastic head this morning – I think it was the Chinese meal last night. Where to go and should I time it – these are my immediate concerns as I leave the house. Well, original as ever, it's up Browfoot, jelly bean and back. Peter rabbit is sitting in the middle of the lane just where I am going to turn. He watches and waits until I get almost up to him, then he bounds off. At the same moment the cuckoo calls out, starting loud and clear, then fading away. Do I frighten the rabbit or does the cuckoo warn him of my approach? There are more engaging thoughts to be had out here than where to turn. At 15 minutes I decide to go on a bit as the legs are slowly coming to life, but it's just bread and butter stuff. I need to get quicker, go further and adopt a more positive mental attitude as the clock is running.

June 4

I feel more decisive this morning. I have a plan. I am going to give the Bowston circle a go, a new route, a different direction. I drove it in the car a while ago; it was well over 5 miles, nearer 6 as I recall and the last section seemed endlessly up, even in the car! So it has lain dismissed in my mind since then. But this morning

I head out through the village and on to the main road towards Kendal. There's lots more traffic than I'm used to but the path is set well back from the road. I bear left for Bowston, up past a handful of houses and a long run downhill, which I can never really enjoy as I'm always thinking what goes down must come up. Also there's a fair amount of cars along this narrow, windy stretch. But once through Bowston, I take a left over the quaint little bridge and lose all the traffic. The lane to Staveley is quiet but for the birds and a cockerel, just a narrow lane being overtaken by luscious green growth. I meet the up section head on, with energy 'blok' in mouth, arms working, focus on something in the bank about 10 paces on, draw that in then find the next focus, trying not to look for the top of the hill or to the endless rise – eyes right. As I approach our house in the distance I take my first look at pedometer. It shows 5.43. At this point I reckon if I take the river path and go back through the village that will take me to a record breaking 6 miles. So that is what I do and arrive home on 6.24 miles – another step closer, elated. I enjoy a

celebratory banana and heartily congratulate myself until I think that less than half a mile further would have taken me over half of the half marathon - deflated!

June 6

It may be D-day out there in the world but it's just another day in the office here. One of those exquisite mornings that have you awake with the birds inviting you to join them, and very loud and persuasive they are too. So it's up relentlessly steep Hawe Lane, known to us as Moaning hill. And moan and groan and puff and pant I do but I get to the top still running, heart still beating (just). A backward glance reveals Staveley well below me now. It's flat along the top, and of course there are eggs out for sale in the little wooden box when I have no money and no bag. Through a couple of gates, carefully over the cattle grid, then it's downhill all the way, which is a bit of a strain on the old knees. Back home the dry stone waller is out repairing our wall. The pedometer reads 3.2miles and my watch says about 40 minutes. I'm not unhappy with that as I regard it as an hour's brisk walk when we go to collect the eggs. So I acknowledge this as proof that I run faster than I walk!

June 9

Oops missed a day's training. Just back from a bridge packed weekend in Kelso. There were places to run but I didn't find the opportunity. We drove there on Saturday and by afternoon the rain was torrential. We drove home today with rain again torrential, but clearing enough for me to venture up Browfoot for half an hour. It really is all I can fit in today. But Laura used to say that any run is better than no run. So, Laura, this is strictly an 'any run', just the start of my build up for Penrith Parkrun on Saturday.

June 11

I've got half a plan for today, no route in mind but a determination to better 6.24 miles. I've been getting lots of advice as I go round trying to boost the DBA coffers. 'Run further' is both common and logical advice, easy to say, 'just another mile or two'. For me it's far more than another mountain to climb. So I set off with pedometer on an unknown destination. I run up to Scroggs Bridge and back just for starters. I note a colony of yellow flag irises along the river bank, and with a wry smile I wonder if they can make their way up stream. I was given some iris tubers in a tub a while ago which I left down on our river bank; but before I got round to planting them torrential rain filled the river, spread to the bank and washed them and the tub clean away. I thought then that one day we would see lots of flag irises further down the river – not up?? Next I make my way through the village and on to the Crook road.

An idyllic rural setting lies before me with a red tractor chugging up and down a distant field, harvesting the grass.

As I have run through the months it has been a revelation to witness Staveley's seasons unfold – from barren to bountiful!

I run on much further this time towards Crook until I see the main road, then I turn to wend my way back (without looking at pedometer). As I approach the village I can't resist a peep – just gone 5.4 miles, it will be over six by the time I get home. I may as well try a few more add ons and make it 8 miles. I take a left turn and run up past Sidegarth and back, a right turn down Ashes Lane, where we nearly bought a house, and back – that's steep. There is a shiny blue helicopter parked in a garden down there. Back through the village, nearly home, eyes now fixed to the pedometer, nearly 7 miles. So it's off up to Scroggs Bridge and back again. 7.5 as I reach home – can't leave it at that, on towards the river walk, up to the gate, turn. As I lurch towards the front door it rolls on to 8.08 miles. No idea of the time, it doesn't matter. One of May's aims achieved, 8 miles of continuous running and do I feel good about that, especially after banana and a shower, I do. Just that nagging doubt - can I add 5 miles to that?

If at first...

JUNE 13

After my 'marathon' effort on Tuesday one leg is a bit achy, so a steady 3 miles is today's aim, and probably postpone Penrith Parkrun tomorrow. I set out along the river, across the meadow, thinking a bit of off roading may be gentler on the legs and a rendition from the Sound of Music, good for the soul. In fact the uneven surface doesn't make it any easier on my leg and there are two gates and a stile to contend with. Back home I receive a call from Flossie at *Westmorland Gazette*. They want to do a story about this old gran running; they are coming to take a photo on Monday, full running uniform!

JUNE 15

A mizzly, warm father's day dawns. I decide to go up towards Kentmere and back along Browfoot, changing the rotation of this circular run. I am surprised to see a colony of tents and cars and bikes dotted around a field. I have never seen anyone camping here before. A sign informs me it's Sam Houghton camping. A huge annual cycling challenge was held around the village yesterday in memory of Sam, who died of cancer, aged 22.

We walked down to the woodyard to watch some of

the exhausted looking cyclists complete the challenge, tired and muddy. Lots of water bottles and bananas, satisfied looking faces, hugs, congratulations. The atmosphere was buzzing down there – what is The Great North Run going to be like? I digress.

I cut through the farm track, alongside a brook. As it is stony and wet, rivers running through the path in places, I decide to walk the half mile through the farm yard and up onto Browfoot – no good risking an injury. A straightforward circular run with no arguments clocks up 4.5 miles in about an hour.

16 JUNE

A no run day. But I get all dressed up disguised as a runner for the photographer from the *Westmorland Gazette*. He has me out in the lane with a pair of trainers round my neck, sitting casually on a tree root, smiling, as droves of people and dogs look on curiously. Then I do a slow motion run towards him. Slow motion running is my speciality!

JUNE 17

John is off to Borrowdale at the break of dawn, doing his Gervase Phinn thing. I've got to prepare for my Penrith thing. It's a warm, muggy morning so I decide to go out early. Nothing ambitious as I have a headache, but I'm hoping a little jog along quiet country lanes will cure it. It doesn't but I manage half an hour and come back very hot and not fancying a banana at all.

Image courtesy of The Westmorland Gazette

June 19

As the sun pours in through open windows, I lie in bed overcome by indecision, vacillation, and hesitation – how far, big one, average, what route, timed, measured?? It's a relief when I actually set off. Today's decision is no timer or pedometer; repeat the circular run of the other day. I think I quite like the fact I have scheduled a compulsory walk in the middle; banish thoughts of Penrith; enjoy the beautiful tranquil morning, weaving in and out of the shade from canopies of trees into dappled light then vivid bright sun. I count five rabbits, a pheasant, lots of hens, cows and sheep, one cyclist, three cars and I hear a cuckoo in the distance. Back home within the hour – one banana waiting and one Parkrun pending.

21 June

Longest day, longest 3 miles! It's Penrith Parkrun day. We are more organised today. We get up in good time for banana and porridge and enjoy the scenic, more leisurely drive over Shap. We arrive in time to have a little look round, a panic and a warm up. I'm busy trying to copy warm up routines of lean looking athletes.

Then it's time for the line up and start. I position myself midfield, though there are a lot less people than last time. And we're off at a cracking pace. I'm going faster than usual but within seconds the entire field is stretching out some way in front of me. Puffing and panicking I realise I must set my own pace and not worry about the race. And so I run on, alone, as the field pull ever further forward. It takes me a while to calm down and realise it's not going to be any easier than last time. As I run around the pavilion, nearing the end of the first lap I notice a chap behind me. All this way and I hadn't realised there was anyone behind me. My surprise is short lived as he accelerates past me at pace and I realise I am being lapped – he is about to finish the race as I embark on my second tortuous lap. He is greeted with applause as he speeds towards the finishing line, and I get some applause too. Should I say 'I'm not second I'm last' but I suspect they all realise this from my speed, age, demeanour and they are just giving me a bit of encouragement and sympathy. From the side lines John calls out 'go a bit faster'. No sympathy or encouragement from him. 'He wants me to die', I think as I lurch on in the hot, bright sunshine.

Anyway another lap there is to run and I can just see the back runners, but I can never come near catching them – not even the lad I noticed walking with a pronounced limp before the race, for he runs with a fast limp and finishes a minute ahead of me. It is with

great relief I cross the finishing line, last, and have my barcode swiped. All the stewards are relieved I've finished as they are waiting to clear up and go home – my nightmare has become a reality and I  realise there are plenty of worse things that can happen. I have succeeded in doing another parkrun, torturous though it may be. I live to run another day, it's for a good cause and I will enjoy it!

On arrival home I check my time on the website and am very disappointed that I am 30 seconds slower than last time. First in my age category, and the one below, is little consolation. I thought this would be easier, that I must be fitter and faster than a couple of months ago, that 3 miles wouldn't seem too far after 8.08 miles, but it wasn't and I wasn't and it didn't!

I could make a little confession here. Back in April John reckoned I cut a corner by not running round some flags on the last lap. This could potentially have added 35 seconds to my time, meaning that I have in fact produced a personal best, some 5 seconds faster than last time (unofficially).

June 23

Beautiful spell of weather we're experiencing. The sun is pouring through the window at 7am. I'm happy to get up and go but where, how, not at all sure whether focus should be on faster or further. I'm still feeling disappointed after Penrith and lacking a smart goal strategy. So, when in doubt Browfoot it is - just a case of job done for today.

June 25

I checked emails before going to bed last night and found there had been 2 donations to Just Giving page – a total of £50. So I planned to run 5+mile circuit round Bowston, worth £10 a mile I told myself.

Armed with a plan I am up and away by 7am, no problem, on a warm nondescript morning. I run along the main road, then turn away, out in to the country,

past Bowston village and further from civilization. As I run along a quiet lane I notice a white van parked in the wood with two men beside it. One of them looks up and my eyes meet his and I mumble, 'morning' as I run silently past. Next I hear the van start up and come towards me. I stand to one side to allow it to pass. It stops just in front of me. My heart is pounding. The driver asks if I'd like a lift but I nervously reply I want to run. One of the men gets out of the van and come towards me, saying I should go with them. I start to run in a panic – should I head into the woods or go back towards the nearest house. I must be able to run faster than the men and the van is facing the wrong way. So I run, faster than I've ever run before.

You've guessed ... me running fast has to be fiction, just one of my imaginary ramblings that kick in whenever I see white vans in quiet places. And there actually is a white van parked in the wood, no men though. My fear passes when I run on and no van is following me.

Onwards. I see my first squirrel of the year run across my path, sadly grey. They can't be as common up here as down south. I see a hen sitting on a stone wall looking somehow incongruous. On arrival home pedometer reads 5.80 miles and timer 74.25 minutes. A sustained slow pace somewhere around 4.5 mph. Today, I'm happy with that.

June 27

Yesterday I was in the Beehive village sell everything shop, when I noticed a large sweet jar of Sports sweets. I had a little paper bag weighed out to try because, to be perfectly honest, I never felt the expensive sweets I got from the specialist sports shop lived up to their names or their grandiose claims – energy, power. So, this morning, with new sweets in my pocket, I set off up Hawe Lane. I choose this route with its uncompromising hill because there is a sign down by the bridge saying ROAD CLOSED EXCEPT FOR ACCESS LONG DELAYS

Long delays on a little lane going nowhere, and seeing about three cars a day – this I have to witness! Anyway, apart from a few newly filled pot holes and a tarmac lorry at the top of 'moaning hill' I see no long delays or even short ones - such is the Cumbrian concept of long delays! No wonder I prefer it up here to down south; they know about delays down there. I do see a little mouse scurry across my path and some newly born black calves. I experience my usual 'never running up here again' struggle to be rewarded by the breathless, breath-taking views from the top. The rest is flat, downhill, flat and home without any long delays.

June 29

The reluctant runner eventually sets off at 11.55, 'wendys' her way around the village, up and down cul-de-sacs, round and round crescents, just trying to stay out for as long as I can make myself, cover as much distance. I'm back home by 12.30. It's going to take more than a banana to get me enthused. I'm never going to achieve my ultimate goal; I can barely even get myself out there. If at first I don't succeed ... I need to come up with planned routes, targets, enthusiasm and drive. I am struggling with motivation and it is only the fund raising that is keeping me approximately on task. Help!

July 1

As June turns to July GNR is getting closer. I'm off up Browfoot with pedometer on 3 mile circuit, leaving the timer ticking by the front door. The sky forms a cloudless blue background to the stark mountain tops. Everything below is in shades of green. By contrast I remember the snow on the tops, the orange, brown mountains and the skeleton trees back in the winter. What a journey through the seasons this route takes. Running along in pure sunshine, I feel close to boiling point. It's a relief when I reach Scroggs Bridge and enter the shaded archway. I am grateful that the lights have been dimmed and the temperature turned down. Out of the shade  and on to the home straight, I rev up to the engine's full capacity and make a dash for our door – grab the timer, 38.27. It's always about the same, when I manage to get everything working, but I'm not usually so hot. A nice chunk of cold pineapple, water, banana , shower and I am chilled.

July 3

Having decided I need a bit more umph and motivation in my training if I am to succeed I wonder if perhaps I should get an app that I have just read about. It's called Zombies Run! I look it up. I learn that every time I go for a run I'll hear a chapter of a story. I'm given a runner number, as if in a computer game. A disembodied voice will tell me to pick up medical equipment or food. Then there are the drama bits when the Zombies chase me and I have to run fast. It doesn't say what happens to me if I'm not able to run fast. Could this be the inspiration I need? On further consideration I conclude no, this is not for me. Since I ended my affair with Laura I have enjoyed having nothing electronic in my ears or my head. There are plenty of mesmerising sounds to be heard, and thoughts to be thought.

I do the allotted 40 minutes today in indifferent weather, taking an indifferent route around the village at an indifferent speed. I seem to have reached a bit of an indifferent crisis. Inspiration I need you!

The Running Postwoman

July 5

After much consideration I decide to be a jolly postman this morning – kill two birds with one stone – do a running delivery. I'm having a drop-in day at home next week in aid of Diamond Blackfan Anaemia, so need to get invites posted all around Barley Bridge. With pedometer set, off I go with a pile of envelopes. Finding letter boxes or even front doors isn't always easy. With 3 miles covered at a run and most of my letters posted I have a little stop and quite a big chat with former neighbours up Brow Lane. Then my next delivery across the road to Bridge House necessitates another stop for another coffee and a chat. This is not running as BUPA intended but it makes for an enjoyable morning, which is what I need if I am to get my mojo working. I definitely prefer social running!

8 July

I missed a day of training yesterday as we were visiting the parents. I'm off early this morning to make amends. My aim is for 40 minutes 'pace running' as recommended on several of the training programmes; every time I slow down, I try and speed up, is my understanding of the term. I suspect there is a more technical interpretation. The lanes feel very tranquil this morning. It's rained overnight after a fairly dry spell and the river is looking and sounding much perkier, and everywhere is green, so very green, and fresh. Many of the verges have been given short back and sides. Others are beginning to loll over, heavy with growth and rain. Some beautiful bell flowers catch my eye, yellow rising out of green, also a bright blue flower with delicate petals stands tall. So striking are they we return later with car and camera. As I near the end of my run, hot and puffing, I notice a light rain spray gently cooling and refreshing me. I could order some of that for the 7th September.

July 10

An hour's run is what my new schedule suggests. I plan to go up Kentmere valley and back along Browfoot for the circuit run. But the valley road is so well screened from the warmth of the sun by a thick leafy canopy I decide to turn at Ulthwaite Bridge and retrace my steps – that's how warm it is at 8 o'clock this morning. My heart does miss a beat when I hear someone running up behind me, but he is so quickly past me and out of sight that it is only the one beat missed. A white van then approaches me but as it drives past I note the Open Reach logo and feel safe. It's unmarked white vans that get my imagination doing overtime. I can't find an inspiring story to lose myself in today. Back home I clock myself in at 68mins, hot and thirsty and not a banana to be had, just H_2O.

12 July

I'm getting lots of supportive donations through Just Giving, by post, by hand and in person. When I don't feel like running I have to remind myself of how much family, friends, organisations, neighbours are doing to support me and the cause and I'm off in a flash – well not quite a flash! Such is the case this morning as the jolly postwoman sets out once more armed with Drop-in Day invitations to post from one end of the village to the other. I particularly want to post them up Browfoot because it has been my main route for the last 6 months. I've watched houses wrapped up under frosty roofs, to windows thrown wide open; gardens, dead and buried coming to life and rejoicing with colour. I've measured my progress on which house or farm I get up to and in how long, can I get to the next farm before I turn. I may have passed these buildings many times but finding front doors proves a challenging task. Still, it's something different and I'm on the move.

Postings complete, without social chat and coffee stops this morning, I run back through the village to see what's happening as it is Staveley Carnival weekend. The field car park is already filling up, but thankfully the waist high grass has been cut. As I run through the wood yard I see florescent stewards, the start/finish posts for the Dual Dash race around the village. I hear the steel band warming up. The park looks full of activity, colour, tents and anticipation. What a beautiful hot morning; I hope it holds out for grand procession tomorrow.

July 14

The weather did hold out for the carnival yesterday: the procession and floats presented a cacophony of noise and colour, brilliant. The bunting all around the village looks redundant this morning and an air of calm has returned to Staveley.

I have a forty minute stint planned for today in fine, warm weather. Browfoot for 20 minutes, turn, back, the usual. As I approach the high point enjoying a crystal clear view, one of the clouds turns grey and heavy, shrouding the tops, and leaving an indistinct border between land and sky. What a contrast in the blink of an eye. At least I am home in an unremarkable time before the rain starts and quickly develops. Lots of baking to be done – it's drop-in day tomorrow. I hope the jolly postwoman is happy with the turnout.

Extra, extra, read all about it

July 16

I can't ask for warmer support than I'm getting. It's time to crash through the 10 mile barrier; I've rested on the 8 miles for long enough. Once I've given myself a target and a route I'm motivated. Armed with pedometer and sports sweets I set off with enthusiasm and optimism on a drizzly, cooler day. A new running route takes me up the Crook road and off to the right following the Dales Way. I check my split distance at this point only to see I've forgotten to press the start button on the pedometer. Urghh! Still, I know it's about a mile and I can run back and measure it later– no harm done to my record breaking attempt, onward. I approach a gate with a threatening notice: Warning Cows with calves can be aggressive I can't go under it, can't go over it, got to go through it (in the words of my grandchildren's favourite story). So, how much faster can I run, I wonder, as I enter the dangerous territory. I try to avoid eye contact with the cows, but through the corner of my eye I can see them watching me through the corner of their eyes. It is with relief that I close the second gate, still in one piece. I'm then confronted by a relentless climb over Brackenthwaite; my heart is pounding as I attempt my slow motion ascent. I am reminded of mice on the uphill treadmill and a conversation yesterday with one of my visitors. I was impressed at some of the routes she ran but she informed me that she walked up steep hills and ran the rest. I had viewed slowing to a walk as a crime against running, but why, I now wonder. Better to arrive home alive than to die on a hill or need an electronic pacemaker. So I hereby confess to walking a relatively short section.

The view at the top is rewarding – almost 360°, though not the clearest of days. From here on it is a gentle downhill traverse all the way. Arrival back in Staveley shows me at about 6.4 miles and the fine mist has turned to rain. I run back up to the signpost for The Dales Way, where I started the pedometer, that confirms a mile plus the repeated mile. That takes me back to the village on 8.4, so I do another circuit of the village with all the optional extras, pass the house again, hot, sweaty-wet and rain-wet, down to the river, turn, pedometer clicks over to 9 miles as I stumble, trip towards our house,  and for 9 read 10; I like to complicate these matters. Big milestone reached, headline news 10 miles run, almost continuous. Bring on The Bear Hunt challenge!

Any excuse

July 20

I missed two days of practice due to any number of factors keeping me well occupied. Anyway I think the body needed a bit of a wind-down after its 10 mile, nearly half marathon, adventure. I'm just going for a standard 3 mile run today, starting with the river path.

It's the Beer Festival weekend at Hawkshead Brewery in the Mill Yard and the village was buzzing when we drove through yesterday. I could hear live music drifting through our open windows when I went to bed last night. But at 8am this morning the wood yard sleeps peacefully. On out of the village wild flowers in grassy verges are dying back while blackberries are fighting their way forward. I have just 7 more weeks to jog through the life and seasons of Staveley. Can I keep it going in the face of so much negativity?

July 22

We appear to be in the middle of a heatwave at the moment and got family staying. The plan is to drive up to Kentmere, walk up the valley to the reservoir, picnic in the shadow of the Horseshoe, back along valley bottom, then race the car home, four miles. In the event it is the hottest day of the year, so after a 7.86 mile walk,

I am forced to call off the race and catch the car back home. A walk is going to have to suffice for today. Surely that ranks as a legitimate excuse.

July 24

We are getting as many hot sunny days now as we had wet ones earlier on. A perfunctory run ticking off 3 miles before setting out for Scarborough sounds easy but it remains hard and it's all I've got time for. Someone asked me at what point I hit the wall in a run. Thinking about that this morning I decide the wall is permanently 3 inches in front of my nose. I hit it on every step, good views to the sides though!

July 26

We're in Scarborough for our annual pilgrimage to the Northern Bridge Congress. Hot though it is I need to fit in a jog which I do. As I go to record my jog log I encounter an out pouring of words in utter contrast to my usual scenic, solitary sorties. So I write them all down, they seem to want to rhyme!

July 29

Excuses for yesterday – we got home late from Scarborough. I'm off before breakfast this morning to make amends. It is a cooler day with some rain around from last night. There is a fresh smell of cut grass in the air. I do my usual run against the clock, feel the usual disappointment on arrival home, clock showing about 37 minutes for 3 miles. Watching the Commonwealth

Saturday morning & a run through sunny Scarborough

Run through streets of tall houses, hotels, B & Bs
Towards cliff top, snaking path, squirrels around trees
And beyond it all, sparkling views of the sea.
The old bathin' pool and dilapidated Spa tell a story
Like The Grand Hotel in faded Victorian glory.
Run right in to a consciousness stream
Like waking up, yet still in a dream.
Wheel chairs, push chairs, mobility scooters and sticks
Ice cream, hot dogs, fizzy drinks and chips.

Jog, dodge, puff, weave.

Arcades, steel bands, fun fairs and muffled noise
Donkeys, wind breaks, sandcastles and beach toys.
Ambling, sitting, shopping and browsing
Talking, texting, sunbathing and drowsing.

Run, dodge, puff, weave

Big dogs, little dogs, terriers and pit-bulls
Circling, squawking, everywhere, seagulls.
Sun hats, wrinkles, bald heads, grey heads
Fluorescent pinks, yellows, greens and reds
Bodies white, tanned, flesh wobbling through,
Cigarettes, mobile phones, ring tones, tattoos.

Jog, dodge, pant, weave.

Run past the harbour on along North Shore,
Quieter, run further, but no time for more
Turn, hot, sweaty, head back to B&B
Back through the chaos, sparkling views of the sea

Puff, weave, run, relax

Games it occurs to me I want my time to improve with each run, which of course it never does or will. Resolution: to be more precise in my timing, to lower my expectations and to set more realistic goals. These athletes deal in fractions of a second, while I'm vague about the minutes.

July 31

Not sure if my goal for today is realistic; it is certainly not worth timing. I have mapped out a new route which means conquering the summit of Browfoot, then dropping down to Ings and back along the main road and newly surfaced level pavement. This has become a more realistic proposition since I realise I can break into a walk when I simply can't run another step up and my heart is about to require a pacemaker. However, as I approach Browfoot Farm a dark grey cloud enshrouds the surrounding fells and drops of rain begin to fall. I have no rain coat so I adapt my plan to return via Ulthwaite Bridge and Kentmere road as it is arched by a thick, verdant canopy which might afford me some shelter. In the event the cloud disperses and the sun makes a weak attempt to break through, so I could have carried on, rather than come up with a convenient excuse, not that it seemed like an excuse at the time. I arrive home warm and dry, just over 4 miles on pedometer. And I already know my route for Saturday.

August 2

A new month dawns; I can almost touch September

now. It is pouring with rain this morning so I wait until it looks a bit brighter then make my move. I set out about 3pm for the big challenge – can I run to

the top of Browfoot and live to tell the tale? Well, I come, I see, but I don't conquer. I walk the last 0.2 of a mile, so I almost conquer. I just can't keep going round bend after bend, up after up, even though I get the best 3D view in the house of the Lake District at its stunning best, hills, fields, stone walls, rocky crags, valleys, sheep, tranquillity. Once at the top the track is rougher than I'd remembered and puddles linger from overnight rain. Three Herdwick sheep stand blocking my path, a mother and two dark grey lambs, watching, waiting. As I get almost level with them I back into the wet bracken, right up against the wall so they can pass

me. That would be too easy. They stop and there we all stand, looking at each other, motionless. Finally I decide I have better things to do, I'm supposed to be running, not standing around waiting for sheep to pass. So I make my move, upon which they do an about turn and set off in my direction, walking first, then running, acting as pacemakers, me, with no option but to follow, until they finally turn off the track into a field.

Alone again, I continue picking my way through stones and puddles. A strange, rumbling sound turns out to be an imminent threat of rain, big, heavy, cold drops, slow at first, then fast and furious. No place to shelter, bleak and exposed, I keep running, dripping, splashing. No coat, no hat, no wipers for my glasses, totally exposed to the hostile elements. I am somewhat relieved when the track turns to tarmac, rain bouncing back off it, and civilisation is back in sight. I'm not sure which path to take when I reach a crossroads. There's no one silly enough to be out and about, no one to ask. I choose the widest track as I want to get on to the main road as quickly as possible before I drown or freeze!

As I approach the main road at Ings the rain disappears without a rumble and a brazen sun barges through. Only soaking clothes, dripping hair, speckled glasses, sploshy trainers, spraying cars, splashy puddles act as reminders of the water torture that has just been inflicted on me. As I arrive home, still soaking wet through and through, weather ironically fine, I note 6.2 miles on the pedometer. Not a run I'll be repeating, though maybe it would have created a better impression without the cold water power shower half way round. I shouldn't have found an excuse to call it off last time. The banana is relegated as a hot shower tops the homecoming agenda.

August 4

I am truly hopeless. I settle for a timed 3 mile run against the clock on a bright, sunny day, in complete contrast to yesterday. I definitely make a quicker start than usual. But when I check for distance I realise that, in my determination to set off the timer at the last minute, I'd forgotten to start the pedometer. Still, I can accurately check that distance later, so, on up to Scroggs Bridge at a bit of a gallop and turn. Back through the village in the other direction. As I pass the weir at Wilfs a loud roar confirms how all that torrential rain has renewed its strength and energy. The river is up and running with its frothing head held high. Meantime my energy is running out and Saturday's rain did nothing to restore it! Home is in sight but the pedometer reveals I'm short on distance, so its back down toward the river path , turn and try again, 1234. The timer I left running at home shows 35.34 which I would be happy with but for the fact I'm not sure of my exact distance – to be confirmed later. What I need is a backup team. I bet Mo has one.

August 6

I'm not proud of today's running efforts. It is very wet this morning so I put off my run until afternoon. I do however, have a rewarding morning collecting prizes for the DBA charity raffle from local business/shops, and in so doing I get told about a programme which helps plan and time routes, working out distance once you key in the starting point. I think it's called Run Routes.

By the time I finally get going I am in a rush and do just one circuit of the village, one mile, any excuse, as fast as I can – don't actually record the time but I am well puffed. Surely one mile should be well within my capabilities. Well it doesn't feel like it today.

August 7

Georgie and Co. arrive about 8pm after five hours of tests at hospital following Heidi's referral to St Mary's Paddington – long hard day for them, but as usual, no complaints. I am busy settling everyone in and even doing a bit of cooking on Friday with no time for a run.

August 9

I know I have to make time to go out today, so when the family go off to the aquarium, I seize the moment, don my running gear and am off in a flash, well, something

a bit more akin to a whimper. 40 minutes at reasonable pace and I am back home getting the evening meal ready for a big family gathering with Dan and Adele joining us.

Just to remind me how close The Great North Run is getting the postman arrives with a DBA T-shirt and running vest, and an information pack with my number, 54519, and starting colour, pink, which I note is right at the back. I read with horror that by now I should be comfortable running 8 miles. I just thought I had to do it, no one mentioned comfort. I'm not comfortable running full stop. The number apparently relates to your expected finishing position. They've obviously got a lot of faith in me then! All this stuff would have to arrive when I'm preoccupied with Meg and Heidi, family, cooking. I'm so keen to absorb all the information to anticipate the day but now is not the moment. A cursory look and it's stored away for later.

On this same day it is reported on the news that Mo Farah will be leading the elite race; hardly fair for him to start in front of me. Still how amazing is it to be running somewhere in his wake, and with Seb Coe as the starter. I get quite excited when I think about it, then reality kicks in, followed by panic.

Forget running, everyone is waiting to be fed.

11 August

We've spent a lovely day out and about with the children, on the go in the sunshine.

I force myself out this evening after story-time and with limited reserves of energy. It's drizzly but warm. Round and round the village with a few extensions I wend my weary way, with my legs trying to keep up with my feet, and my head some way behind, stumble, trip, stumble trip. Whatever the excuse this is not good preparation for next week's 13 miles but as Laura has said before, 'Any run is better than no run.' I seem to take comfort from this quote on many an occasion. And I assume half a banana is better than no banana as that is all I can face when, with relief, I arrive back home.

14 August

I left an eerily quiet house this morning, having dropped Georgie and the girls off at a friend's house in Manchester yesterday. Weather is warm and sunny. Again I decide to run as far as Goose Howe as I am feeling generally weary, then I think of Heidi and all they are going through with such stoicism, and I feel compelled to push myself further and stop making excuses and whinging about being tired. I continue on to Browfoot Farm, through to Ulthwaite Bridge and back along the Kentmere Road. As I am nearing home I feel a few spots of rain dripping through the arch of trees. The sky is still bright. I anticipate a rainbow but see none. By the time I reach home the sky has turned

dark, the rain is heavier and I am just starting to get wet,
an almost perfectly timed finish.

Master Plan

I set off for the Bowston round run today, about 5.6 miles. I am going to try 13 miles this week, that is the master plan, 13 whole miles, so I need to up my game. I start the pedometer and timer as I leave the house and head towards the main road on a grey drizzly day. The verges that have not been cut back are looking particularly lanky and scruffy. Nettles, grasses and brambles dominate. It appears to me that the countryside is not at its best in August. The excitement of summer is fast fading, the green is tarnished and autumn, with its glorious colours, is waiting around the next corner. I catch unwanted glimpses of squashed animals, birds, slugs. Today I see the first conker lying in the lane encased in lime green prickles. It would seem to be a good year for cob nuts and acorns are appearing.

Time passes in a haze as section after section of the route is completed without me noticing. That's the thing about a round route, it's non-confrontational. 77 minutes later, according to the timer, I arrive home. According to the pedometer I have done 3.1 miles. I know this is wrong, my route is over 6 miles. I find this pedometer unacceptably sloppy and want to jump on it.

August 18

We had a fantastic three course meal last night in Windermere to celebrate our wedding anniversary, so I need to run it off today. Mornings are beginning to feel cooler. Soon I shall need to start off with a second layer. How many layers to wear was such a problem back in the winter.

BUPA plan for today is 40 minute run. So I decide on 3 miles against the clock. I run up Browfoot and back in 37.20min. That puts me at about 2hr 48min for half marathon, supposing I keep up this pace when multiplying by over four. Surely this is not possible. My ultimate aim/dream will be to get under 3 hours. Correction – that is a subsidiary aim. My main aim is to complete GNR, hopefully by running all the way.

August 20

On yet another bright, sunny morning I set off up the Moaning Hill torture circuit, convinced it must get easier as I progress with my training. It doesn't. Perhaps this is because I have developed a dry cough and slightly laboured breathing over the past couple of weeks, and being such a finely tuned athlete, this could be affecting my performance! I manage to just keep running up and up, telling myself I need to dig deep. Then it occurs to me that years of erosion have thinned the depths and I only have shallows left to dig in to. Anyway, once at the top a beautiful blue sky with soft white clouds, artistically scattered, awaits me. But no time to stand

and stare. The lane levels out along the top, then, as a cheerful couple walking their dog in the opposite direction tell me 'It's downhill all the way from here.' So it's an easy run back and only seven more runs to go and counting.

A trip to the Doctors reveals a mild chest infection, so, as a doctor, he gives me performance enhancing drugs (antibiotics) and as a one-time competitor in Great North Run, he advises me to complete 13 miles before the actual race so psychologically I will know I can do it, which of course has yet to be QEDed (quite easily done!). He felt when he reached 11 miles he was unsure he could finish as he was yet to do that distance. I think, like him, I will need that reassurance. Others say the adrenalin on the day will see me through to the end.

August 22

There was rain all day yesterday, but it is bright again today with lots of puddles still in evidence. Nothing too ambitious this morning as the master plan is to be executed on bank holiday Sunday. I take the usual route up towards Browfoot and for the first time observe that Reston Scar, which lies behind Heather Cottage, is covered in heather, large swathes of blue scattered randomly on the fell side, reminiscent of bluebells in the spring. I'd always thought, without giving the matter any deep or meaningful attention, that the cottage must have been named after someone called Heather. Noting the heather again on my return trip, I wonder how I have failed to see it before. My eyes and ears are most likely drawn towards the river on the other side of the road, which is both gushing and sparkling due to the rain and the sun.

As I return over Barley Bridge a lorry turns from the other direction. I expect him to stop on the bridge, as that is a drop off point for deliveries to Kentmere Ltd., but this huge lorry is following me across the bridge. He asks if he's on the right road  for Kentmere. I inform him he'll have to reverse his huge articulated lorry back over the bridge and go on up to Scroggs Bridge. He asks if I can hold up the traffic on the road for him while he reverses out. Risking life and limb I hold up 2 cars while he performs this tricky manoeuvre. What adventures I have when just out for a quiet jog round the lanes!

August 24

Bank Holiday Sunday – t'was to be the BIG ONE, the master plan, but on Friday night I was woken with a nerve pain down my side, right leg from hip to knee. It got worse as Saturday progressed. I diagnosed myself with sciatica, tried to cure it with ice, heat and ibuprofen, but it kept on getting worse. I struggled to sit down, stand up, and stairs were a real problem in both directions. I knew there was no way I could run on Sunday, though when I wake I am in less pain than on Saturday, helped by dosing up with ibuprofen.

We decide, as it's such a lovely day we'll try walking to the Sheep Show in Kentmere. It's never worth getting the car out on a fine bank holiday, unless you like sitting in it. I manage the walk, just experiencing discomfort on ups, downs and uneven stretches, sitting isn't easy either. In fact walking seems to be about the best thing I can do. As I walk along these familiar running routes it occurs to me what a pleasant and social activity walking is. John will accompany me on a walk and I have spare breath to talk and time to 'stand and stare.'

Doctor Mike visits in the evening to deliver some plums and gets called upon for a professional diagnosis. He confidently pronounces that I have trochanteric bursitis, not sciatica, due to excessive running. I'm all right with the Latin diagnosis, sounds an impressive reason not to run but I'm not so enamoured with the common garden term, housemaid's knee, in my hip. It requires similar treatment to my diagnosis but may require an injection as I need to get it sorted quickly and will need a doctor's appointment on Tuesday. Why have I never heard of an athlete with housemaid's hip? What a blow to my schedule; I was so geared up for the 13 mile Grasmere gallop. Cross fingers and toes that it's not a blow to the 7th September.

August 26

After a day of very light exercise I am pleased to wake with nothing more than a twinge in my right hip, so forget the doctor for now. There is a slight autumnal feel to the weather this morning and I can see it's windy, so it's back to long sleeves for today's run. But my real conundrum is how far to go with my schedule damaged. I really want to run 13 miles before GNR but I don't want to take any unnecessary risks and time is no longer on my side. I opt for the usual village circuit then up Browfoot. Once out there I realise I am wrong about autumn. Bright sun, warmth, every shade and texture of green topped in clear, cloudless blue. I am passed

by a cycling mother with two children, one on a side car attached to her bike, the other independent on her own little bike. They remind me of Meg and Heidi. I pass them later picking blackberries. They're still picking them when I am on my return leg and proudly show me a half full container.

Back via the village our paths cross again; they're on their way home and so am I. Forty-five minutes run, hip and leg moving, a sigh of relief, so it's on with the revised master plan.

August 27

John is off early to do his 'Gervase Phinn training' and I'm suffering no after effects from yesterday's outing. I really want to get this big run out of the way as soon as possible. The original idea was for John to drop me off in Grasmere, 13 miles away, and for me to run home. He had worked out all the distances on the Run Route programme. I consider getting the bus there but we intended to check footpaths around Rydal as it's such a busy stretch of road. So I decide on a compromise plan. I will run round the village, 1 mile, up to Kentmere Church, 4 miles, on towards the reservoir, about a mile depending on steepness and path quality, and back, approximately 12 miles in total.

It is a lovely day yet again as I don the race day gear for a full and final dress rehearsal – new sports bra and pants, capris, DBA vest, fluorescent pink marathon socks, L & R, the full September 7 kit, bar my number and foot tag – a vision in lycra. I think back to that cold winter's day when I ordered a baggy T-shirt to team up with my track suit bottoms. I didn't know all this high tech running gear existed.

I start the pedometer, two sports sweets in my pocket and I'm away. It's not until I get past Ulthwaite Bridge, past the factory that the valley suddenly opens out. This is new running territory. I had forgotten how

breath-takingly stunning the panoramic view is, farm houses dotted around the valley bottoms and lower slopes below the dramatic, towering crags of the horse-shoe. I can even make out my next target in the far distance, St Cuthbert's church at the head of the valley, all there in a single glance under a clear blue sky.

I make my way along the lane with the church growing in stature. Up a steep bank around the church I manage to pick the odd juicy blackberry as I pass. I carry on towards the reservoir, through a gate and on to a track. I see Kentmere Hall to my left with its 14th century pele tower and envisage the Border Reivers invading over Mardale to grab any livestock, while the

locals herded them into the safety of the hall. This is a backdrop almost unchanged throughout the long course of history. How privileged am I to live in such surroundings. I want to run as far as I can into the valley before I turn because I'm on about 5 miles now. The trouble is the track keeps rising and the midday sun is so hot I strip down to my sports bra. I promise myself if it's level around the next corner I'll carry on. It isn't, I turn. I'll have to try and do some extra at the other end. This is why I wanted to be dropped off somewhere with no choice but to run home, thus avoiding the internal conflict – to turn or not to turn. This lady always seems to be for turning!

Coming back, in spite of a fresh wind, my legs are beginning to feel heavy, especially when cars appear and I have to stop, squash myself up against a wall or bank avoiding nettles and brambles, then start up again. As I finally approach home I drag myself past the bridge, through the village and back along the river, thus passing my 10 mile barrier. I reach the door at 10.5 miles and there is no way my legs will make that up to 11 by running on. I remember the doctor's advice, and that from several other aspiring runners. I so want to run on, to complete at least 12 miles but the opposition from feet, legs and brain is too strong. They think it's all over, 2 hours 35 minutes is enough, but I know it's not. Another 2.6 miles to find– and if I am ever to find it now, it will have be in Newcastle.

It's the final countdown

August 29

There appear to be no repercussions from Wednesday's Kentmere canter. With four more runs to go, I opt for 30 minutes today as flat as I can make it, but trying to add a couple of bursts of speed. I venture out in the afternoon as the sun puts in an appearance. The lanes are littered with beech nuts crunching underfoot and bits of broken twigs, portents of autumn.

August 31

There is car boot in the village today and it's a lovely sunny morning, so I have to go and support that. In fact it's so warm I leave my fourth to last run until later on in the afternoon. I try to set off at a reasonable pace but within 4 minutes I have stitch. I don't think I've had that since Jersey and it serves as a timely reminder not to eat too close to going out. I slowly run through it and manage to persuade myself not to turn round. I'm quite impressed how the active side of me just manages to override the sedentary side. 'Well done!', I say to myself as I take the longer route back. I said the same on Tuesday when I passed St Cuthbert's Church, because I never thought I'd do that. I'm still very disappointed though, that I couldn't manage the 13 mile planned route last Sunday. Quite a lot of the advice out there suggests I should do the long run today but the BUPA plan said to do it 2 weeks before. I don't feel there is enough recovery time for me.

There is an interview with Mo Farah, who's 'in it to win it', in the paper today giving out some training tips for Great North Run competitors, for me. I absorb all his advice as, quite remarkably, I'm running in the same race as iconic Mo. I need to start 'carb loading' soon, and drinking lots of water, before, not during the race. The really worrying tip is make training pleasurable – HOW? The pleasurable bit is when it's done. Still not long to go now.

September 2

Last night I was informed I had been sighted in Kentmere, bare mid-riff, standing still, twice. I had to point out I was only standing still, squashed against the wall, because they were driving past me ... twice!

And so to third-to-last run and counting down. It is a sunny day in September; suddenly a day like this seems precious, as though we are in remission from autumn.

No worries about layers. I set pedometer and timer. Basically I want to know if I can cover more ground in 40 minutes than I could a month or two ago. As I turn at the

top I feel relieved that this run is now downhill and there are just 2 more to go. A slight wind causes the leaves to rustle through the natural arch of trees, adding to the sound of water tumbling over the rocks. In the shade I try to push on and arrive home with pedometer at 3.3 miles and timer showing 41min.10sec. I never quite manage to get a straight comparison, in fact it's rare for me to set both devices off properly, but I think it's all much the same throughout – no startling world records, no earth moving beneath my feet! But I'm still running and the end is in sight – two to go on the final countdown.

September 3

I know I did a run yesterday, well it was so pleasurable I decided to run again today (I wish). Real reason ... I want my ultimate run before the Great North Run to be on Friday. Today I have a plan; I'm going to be abandoned. A mere drop in the ocean compared to my Grasmere plan. It is a mild day, slightly overcast when John drops me off in Windermere. He wants to drop me off at the bottom of the lane leading to the main road; I insist he drops me off at the top. There are quite enough ups on the main road. Once out there the run is better than I had imagined, as there is only really the one big long hill. With so much traffic whizzing past it takes me about 2 minutes to cross over the dual carriage at Ings. I am not surprised to see a dead badger lying on his back on the grass verge, legs up in the air. Who couldn't prefer the serenity of Browfoot? Still, with the word 'penultimate' sounding in my ears I check pedometer as I arrive home, 4.06 miles, the timer shows 52 minutes. Closer analysis tells me that's 13 minutes a mile, which would put me under three hours. However, it will be a very different story trying to sustain that sort of pace for three times further than today +1.1 miles, very different indeed!

Coincidentally there is a picture of Boris Becker in the paper today. The headline reads **Tennis elbow? No, Boris has housemaid's knee**. According to Consultant surgeon at the Royal Orthopaedic Hospital, Birmingham *'Boris has a nasty case of olecranon bursitis – the elbow version of housemaid's knee.'* That's made me feel better about my housemaid's hip – I'm in illustrious, sporting company!

September 5

The final training run and what a beautiful day for it. I feel demob happy, no pedometer, no timer. Where else could I go but up Browfoot, my training ground for the last seven months. Just to add a touch of celebration/relief to the occasion the Staveley chronicler is out and about with her camera, popping up here and there recording the final circuit. There are so

many milestones along this route that I have struggled to reach, before facing the next challenge, the next struggle. I reflect that although it never seems easy, if I think back to the early days of *Couch to 5K* I am able to run a lot further and a bit faster. The progression has been slow, so slow that it's sometimes been barely detectable, but today I am able to recognise it and it feels good. Jogging along in the sun this morning is pleasurable, so Mo is right, it can be. As I approach Barley Bridge and home I decide to do a final lap of the village, my very own secret lap of honour and I enjoy every moment of it. Back home John has a chopped banana in a bowl of porridge waiting – bring on the carbs, bring on Newcastle.

SEPTEMBER 6

This marks the beginning of the end of my new year's resolution. We set off for Whitley Bay, having gone through my check list: running gear, marathon socks, puffer, race number, safety pins, sports sweets, joining instructions. My sole focus is on Sunday. If there was a time to chicken out of this run, I've missed it by many months. The training is done, the money raised. If ever a person had a reason to run it's surely me, surely now.

As we approach Newcastle, there are banners along the road side welcoming runners. We find our glorified seaside guest house, which although a 30 minute metro ride from the Great North Run start, is full of runners. The metro is advertising special GNR tickets. An electronic arrivals board is intermittently flashing up 'good luck to GNR runners'. Everything has something to do with tomorrow's big event.

We take a trip into Newcastle to watch the City Games which, I had wrongly concluded, would be right in the middle of the city centre. I had also wrongly assumed everyone would know about them. By the time we find our way to the quayside, stopping to watch some younger runners, the games are just finishing, but we get a flavour, a very mild flavour I imagine, of what is to come. Tension is mounting.

Great North Run

'Only those who risk going too far can possibly find out how far one can go.' T.S.Elliot

September 7

Seagulls announce the dawning of the big day, a bright and sunny one, following on from a sleepless night. The order of the day for breakfast from all the runners is bananas and porridge. So of course they are out of them and we have to wait for more porridge to be made, no bananas to be had. Talk is of times, achieved and desired. Dress is vests, lycra trousers or shorts and trainers, except for Elvis who wears her white bejewelled suit and saves her big black wig for the run. I have no appetite but I want to fuel my body so I wade through half a bowl of lumpy porridge and a glass of water.

Then it is on the metro to Newcastle City Centre. The atmosphere is buzzing. Runners approaching the platform from every direction, fancy dress, bright colours, numbers pinned to the front, time chips attached to trainers. On to a train already full of runners, nine stops to Haymarket, and at every station more runners pile in. With our destination reached all the squished and squashed runners erupt on to the street, to join still more runners heading for the start. We become part of a surging mass, which decide as one to visit the long line of portaloos.

Twenty minutes later we arrive at the start but from there, zone A for elite athletes, we have to make our way through the alphabet for over 1k , passing 36 double decker baggage buses, appropriately colour coded, to zone K. Numbers are allocated in accordance with predicted time. Mine is 54519, not too much official expectation riding on my shoulders, but a lot of sponsorship money, good wishes and personal pride. Colour coded numbers allow admittance to the corresponding zone. I say goodbye to John and enter Pink Zone K (the very back) with fear and trepidation. I weave my way forward as best I can. I have memories of Penrith Parkrun where I started at the back and within 10 minutes was so far behind I could barely see the rest of the field. Running at the back is quite a concern for me; I go through any amount of other concerns as we wait in the sunshine. I am surrounded by people I don't know, young people, fit looking, relaxed, and noise. Loud speakers are all along the route issuing a running commentary of happenings further up the line, naming all the visible charities, leading a warm up. Overhead on a bridge I pick John out in a crowd with his camera and more remarkably he finds me in a much bigger crowd. I give him my best Wobot, my very own W version of Mo's mobot. At  10.15 the loud speaker calls out names for the wheel chair athletes followed by the elite women. The GNR is underway amidst huge cheers and applause. The Red Arrows fly over to mark the occasion, another remarkable spectacle of noise, colour, speed. The elite men are introduced next. "Raise the roof off Newcastle – it's Mo Farah" says the speaker. The cheer that goes up from 56000 runners and however many spectators joining together in one voice must come close to achieving this feat. It is one of those moments when you have to be there to feel the noise and excitement vibrate through your body.

And then the long walk begins as we make our way to the start. I don't feel a need to talk to anyone; within the pink zone I am encased in my own little zone, watching, absorbing, listening, fearing, anticipating. About 40 minutes later and we break into a jog. I look at my watch, nearly an hour behind Mo. He must be nearly due to finish. The noise from the speakers is relentless, reeling off the charities, picking out the costumes: the kitchen sink, camel, fairies, clowns, bears, the chap carrying a bike and ever more. By now we are streaming out over the bridge. My Great North Run has started. I am gratefully aware that I am not at the back and I am in fact overtaking a person or two and I am breathing quite easily, unlike both starts at Penrith.

So I settle down at my usual slow pace, but some people are walking, already. This gives me my first ever bit of race confidence. The crowd are clapping along the route and I hear *"Come on pet, come on Wendy"*. At first I think I must be running close to a Wendy, when it dawns on me my name is printed on my number. Running in a bit of an incredulous daze along the middle of a main city road, surrounded by so many runners, onlookers, buildings, traffic lights, I pass the 1 mile marker and check my watch. Needless to say I have only a vague recollection of the start time, somewhere between, 11.25am and 11.35am. I set myself under 15 minutes for the next mile, but again proceed to forget the time I am trying to register.

More importantly the mile markers are being passed

and I'm still running, still edging forward rather than back, while passing water stations, charity stands, brass bands, well-wishers, even sprinkler shower tunnels. I see all these things, hear all this noise, but remain in my own protective bubble, working on reaching the next mile marker. The sun is beating down; if I see any shade by the side of the road I head for it. I have two leg support bandages on my wrists in case legs or ankles start to ache. They prove useful for wiping perspiration from wet hands and dripping forehead.

I meet the half way marker with a mixture of relief and dread. A bit of a buzz travels along the route as people register they're half way there. A live band playing on the roof of a pub a bit further down the road call out "congratulations, half way there" over their speaker system. They clearly don't understand the significance of being over half way – the half way sign is well back down the road. I almost want to shout and tell them. On towards the 7 mile marker and I'm still running. I look at the watch, forget the time, keep running, think of all those people supporting me, try to work out how much sponsorship I am getting a mile. Make calculations, forget them. On a roundabout 'I could run 10000 miles' is blaring out, or is it walk 500 miles. Whatever, it makes me smile. I catch the beat and find I've connected with the rhythm to provide me with a brief boost of energy and pace. The 8 mile marker is a welcome sight but then my immediate preoccupation becomes the 9 mile marker, how many more to go?

Once I go past the 10 mile flag I know I am entering uncharted territory as I've never done more than 10.6 miles. By now I am feeling dazed, just keeping it to a run, hot. At 11 miles I feel full of doubt. Such a shame I have not been able to do the 13 mile trial run from Grasmere. The advice from the doctor comes to mind 'Psychologically you need to have run it to know you can do it.' I hadn't and I didn't. Others said the atmosphere and the adrenalin would see me through, no worries. But with 2 miles to go I feel the doubts escalating. It is uphill and relentlessly hot. Back in Staveley I would never have considered this a hill, but it is billed as uphill. Steve Cram described this last ascent as a 'ball-breaker' and today, to me, it feels like a mountain. This time when I see the United Utilities van I decide I will go through the shower tunnel. Everyone is stopping in it, or walking, enjoying the cold, refreshing spray. I slow to a walk. That is it. My legs seem to lock in a walking action. They feel twice as heavy as usual. I really want to run, I just can't. And so at around 11.5 miles I walk, not even a quick walk, tired, a bit defeated, hot, uphill, forget the time. Most people around me are walking, trudging on. But I am so disappointed. One of the purposes of all that training is so I can run the whole way, and now I'm walking.

Suddenly someone close by shouts almost hysterically *"I can see the sea"*. A tired sort of cheer goes up all around, lots of encouragement. *"We're nearly there."* *"It's downhill now".* *"Not far to go".* *"We can do it".*

It is the first time I have felt the camarardarie that people have told me about. All our spirits seem to lift as we run towards the sea with a last new surge of energy. I am back on track, running again, passing 12 miles. It is so refreshing, after city and roads to be heading for South Shields beach and the finish line. I am going to make it. With 800m to go I feel this is the time to dig deep, try and do a bit of overtaking. So I try and inject a bit of speed, do a bit of overtaking, but no finishing line in sight, keep running, it can't be far.

Then I see 400m to go. I can't keep this up, slow down and save myself for the last 100m. I had completely underestimated 800m. With 100 metres to go dense crowds are lining the way. I grit my teeth and give it my absolute all, along with most of those around me. Under the finish and the clock shows around 4 hours, I check my watch, and have not a clue what any of it means, nor what time I'd started. All I know is that I've finished, I've done it. Woweeee!! I am ushered through a gate and asked for the shoe chip. I know I can't bend down and then get up again, so someone removes it for me. I walk past the stage where Sebastian Coe and Brendan Foster are interviewing the millionth runner. I really want their autograph, but my legs won't wait or take a single unnecessary step. I have to collect my goody bag as I head towards the exit; inside I want to skip and dance – if only!

Bupa great north run

TIME

2:57:59

I have my official photo taken with medal then make my way to the meeting field which is bedecked with letters of the alphabet and to the 'big E' to meet John Ellwood. He greets me with a big hug of incredulity and two bananas. I more collapse on the ground than sit; I remove my trusted trainers and left and right marathon socks, wiggle my toes, put on my tired leg bandages and experience such relief, physical and mental. This challenge has been hanging over me for so long, with all the doubts and uncertainties, the training, the schedules. So many people have sponsored me, so much money, so much support and encouragement. Journey done, finished, no more bananas, no more running. Is any of this real?

All we have to do is get back to the guest house, have a shower, (how I could have wallowed in the jacuzzi in Malta) and relax. It isn't quite as simple as John had planned, due to crowds and queues. Queue, bus, queue, queue, queue, ferry, walk, metro, walk, three hours back to the guest house. The highlight of the journey is finding the GNR results on the phone. My most pessimistic prediction was that I would be right at the back or I simply could not run 13.1m, my feet or legs might collapse or housemaid's hip return. My most optimistic prediction was to finish in under three hours. Official time: 2 hours 57 minutes and 59 seconds! Another Wow! That is such good news, because I am never, ever going to do this run in my life again. I am so chuffed.

My legs may be buried in concrete but my head is in the clouds.

Run for the Money

The fund raising idea came hand-in-glove with the Great North Run. As I registered for the race so I was informed I could open a *Just Giving* page for DBA to help gather sponsorship money. We struggled a bit with the technology but finally got a page, a picture, a story and a background and we were in business. £400 was my original stated target.

In March, once my running plan was well underway, sister, Penny, began mobilising her troops. She was the first one to make a donation on *Just Giving* – to provide the reason to run. This was quickly followed by her family and friends, all leaving wonderful messages of encouragement.

I never really intended to get underway with my fund raising until Georgie, Simon, Meg and Heidi had attended The Diamond Blackfan weekend at the end of May. However just before that the funds got the most tremendous boost when a kind friend from Kendal Bridge Club recommended DBA charity to the Knight Trust, where she was a trustee. I was quite overcome with emotion when they rewarded our efforts with £5000. Following the £5000 donation we were compelled to raise the target. I would have gone to £5400, but John insisted we set our sights higher. £10000 he entered as our new target. I was embarrassed at such an over ambitious and unrealistic target. However, month by month the total grew. Time after time I was dumfounded by people's kindness and generosity

We produced a leaflet in conjunction with Georgie and Simon, setting out information about DBA and the charity, how Heidi is affected by it and my efforts to run a sponsored half marathon. Once this was finalised we proceeded to have it printed in bulk as it was to form the spearhead of our publicity campaign and raise awareness of the condition. It was this same week when Georgie phoned to say "We are supporting the right charity". They had just received a call telling them that genetic testing confirmed Heidi has DBA. It was not the news they, nor any of us, wanted, but in her inimitable way, Georgie absorbs it, accepts it and never complains.

By June it was almost a relief to see our side of family and friends make an appearance on *Just Giving*. And now, armed with the leaflets, I was carrying the campaign into our local bridge clubs at Windermere, Kendal and Grange, where I received tremendous support. I never found asking for sponsorship easy, knowing that everyone has their own causes and concerns and 'limits to their benevolence'. An article I read highlighted this: *Sponsor you? I'd rather run a mile.* In it Claudia Connell recalls the character, Georgie, in the Catherine Tate show, who was forever asking her colleagues to sponsor her in such ventures as, a 5000 mile pedalo race, a fun run dressed as a Cinzano bottle or a two week singathon of Andew Lloyd Webber hits. She would shame them into contributing with made up facts. *'Don't you care that every 38 minutes an OCD sufferer flies home early from their holiday because they think they left the lid off the Shake 'n' Vac bottle'.* Connell also points out that money pledged on *Just Giving* is immediately deducted from the account, regardless of whether the challenge is completed.

I have often wondered when I'm out training whether anyone actually cares whether I run a half marathon or not. The answer is, I care. The GNR is so much more than a running event it is a worldwide platform, allowing me to stand up on the stage and be counted along with iconic athletes and celebrities, to participate and to raise money and awareness.

In my continuing quest for funding I contacted the *Westmorland Gazette* who took a couple of photographs and ran a story headed *'Gran Wendy goes on the run for health charity'* , showing a picture of me with trainers around my neck. Unfortunately this appeared in the local free paper, so didn't attract much publicity. But I used the article and the leaflet to write to organisations that support charities: to Lions, Rotary, all the local groups I could find and was rewarded with a number of generous donations. I was invited to do a small presentation for the Kendal Lions to explain what I am doing, how and why. Clad in my DBA T-shirt, I was warmly received at their  meeting at Kendal Golf Club, where they presented me with a second cheque.

Gran Wendy goes on the run for health group

Half marathon inspired by her granddaughter

by ALLAN TUNNINGLEY

A DEVOTED grandmother is donning her trainers for the first time to take on a half marathon in aid of charity.

Retired Wendy Ellwood, 65, will take on the 13.1 mile Great North Run in September.

She hopes to raise £10,000 for Diamond Blackfan Anaemia, a bone marrow disorder that her two-year-old granddaughter suffers from.

"I've never run in my life but I saw that Diamond Blackfan were looking for volunteers for the Great North Run in December so I started training in January," said Mrs Ellwood, from Staveley.

The mother-of-two's granddaughter Heidi was only diagnosed six months ago with the disorder of the bone marrow.

The bone marrow malfunctions and fails to produce enough red blood cells carrying oxygen to the body's tissue.

"Heidi has struggled since birth - she's never eaten or drank properly and she's very small.

"But she's very bright and still a happy little thing," she continued.

Heidi, who lives in Kent with her father and Mrs Ellwood's 36-year-old daughter Georgie Ashmore, is now waiting for a transfer from Great Ormond Street to St Mary's Hospital, Paddington, for specialist treatment.

Despite starting off with a target of £400, it has now been raised to £10,000 thanks to a £5,000 donation from The Marjorie and Edgar Knight Charitable Trust.

And Mrs Ellwood is already well on her way to target with about £5,406 collected so far.

Having started her fitness programme in January, she is now running at least three miles every other day and has so far reached the eight mile mark, but is pushing for ten in the next month.

"I've got till September 7 to build up to my goal of 15 minute miles," added Mrs Ellwood.

For more information and to donate visit www.justgiving.com/Wendy-Ellwood3

TARGET: Wendy Ellwood is training for the Great North Run

Next I wondered how to rally support in Staveley. I decided to hold a drop-in day for local friends and neighbours. I produced invitations and delivered them in a broad circle around the Old Corn Mill. As well as raising awareness, I took this to be a good opportunity to get to know one or two more of my neighbours.

In preparation for the day I baked cakes and biscuits. The house was eerily tidy as I nervously awaited my first guests. I had a slight panic when I realised I hadn't got a tea pot. I ran next door, no answer. I scoured the cupboards and found a coffee pot – better than nothing. At 11.17 the first guests arrived (so I had got the right day!), and from there a good morning gathering ensued. It went quieter over lunch, but I was never on my own. By afternoon a new group of assembled neighbours enjoyed tea in the garden. By 5 o'clock I was left to reflect on the day. I had invited lots of people I didn't know and was slightly disappointed by the up-take. On the other hand there was generous support for the DBA cause, scones and cake were contributed, plates and cups loaned, gooseberry jam donated for sale, and I certainly got to know some of my neighbours better. I shall enter it as a success with thanks to all who supported me.

The sister had offered to come from Nottingham to help but I rejected the kind gesture as unnecessary, me being such a capable, organised sort of person, albeit without a tea pot! Undaunted she arranged a similar drop-in day a week later for her friends and neighbours, only better organised and with a tea pot. She had a large poster printed which she put up on her entrance door. The weather was great for her garden gathering and lots of money was raised – her final total was £540 – brilliant!

In spite of the fact that I had been so generously sponsored by so many members of the Windermere Bridge Club, I was told their charity evening was to be for DBA. Cakes would be sold and I could run a raffle. I had already written to all the shops/businesses in Staveley requesting sponsorship. A few had sent donations but as many had not replied I took the opportunity to revisit them to request prizes for the charity raffle. This met with a far more enthusiastic response. I came home

laden down after a trip round the Mill Yard – a cycle helmet, which we sold ahead of the raffle, a pack of Hawkshead beer and a gift bag of Cumbrian chutney, a meal for two from Eagle and Child, an epilator from the chemist and a box of biscuits from Spar. I even spread my net a bit wider to cover Morrisons, Booths and Hayes, all of whom willingly offered a prize. Lakeland gave what I considered to be the star prize of a picnic hamper. We landed up with an impressive array of prizes, little and large, donated by a variety of generous people. We sold raffle tickets throughout the week and during the evening which was well attended, with such a lovely atmosphere. People were queuing around the room to buy raffle tickets in generous quantities. We sold 100 more than we had anticipated. A good number of people also donated cakes. At the end of the evening the raffle was drawn then bridge prizes were awarded. I felt warmly supported and indeed I was, with a total of £510 raised to boost the running fund. It was a happy and memorable evening for which I thank the members of Windermere Bridge Club.

As August turned to September the big run day came ever closer and the momentum surrounding it was almost tangible. Good luck cards arrived in the post, through the door, messages of encouragement on email, facebook, phone calls and money still being pledged, some from people I didn't know, some from people I'd never heard of, confounding all our best expectations.

It doesn't matter whether you finish running, ambling or riding on a handcart!! The huge effort you have made and the courage you have shown are an inspiration

Betty
President of Kendal Bridge Club

YOU HAVE RUN A LONG WAY SINCE JANUARY. KEEP GOING WE WILL BE WITH YOU ALL THE WAY - IN SPIRIT!!

PEN AND JOHN

On Sunday, like you, I will run my first half marathon in Chicago in memory of my beloved mum. You can do it, run with your legs and your heart. You can! Eli

Despite the pain of the training and the exhaustion of the event I guess you will reap due rewards for your efforts, in satisfaction in achieving your target in donations and run time and in an unimagined new level of fitness Judy

As you cross the line, we will give you a cheer so loud you will hear it in Newcastle.

Mum and Dad

Armed with all this support there was only one thing to do – run 13 miles.

With master plan successfully executed, money continued to come in and once the last of the sponsorship money was gathered, incredibly 'we' actually reached the unreachable £10000.

Looking back

Seeking information about Diamond Blackfan Anaemia started me off on this unforgettable journey.

My preoccupation over the last 9 months has been getting ready to run and raising money for DBA. I could never have done it on my own; it has been a huge and rewarding team effort.

The euphoria has finally died down. I have been featured in the local paper, twice, I have flashed my GNR T-shirt, sported my medal, proffered my official photos, obtained a short video of me running at vast expense. I've been greeted as a pensioners' hero, telling my story to whoever will listen. And as the dust has settled I've cast the bananas aside, I never did like them, hung up my trainers for good, they're worn out anyway, and pronounced my running days are over.

Have I enjoyed it? is a favourite question. No, is my unequivocal answer, but I wouldn't have missed it for anything. I must be fitter; I'm nearly a stone lighter. It has given me so much satisfaction, warmth, interest, surprise, excitement, euphoria. It has been an amazing, unforgettable experience from the beginning through to the climactic end. The sheer size and scale of the Great North Run, its worldwide reputation, the excitement it generates have helped raise both money

and awareness for DBA as well as creating a life lasting memory for this 'Gran on the Run'.

As for the real raison d'etre, the reason to run: to help fund breakthrough research, to offer hope and support to the DBA family and closer to home, to Heidi, to Georgie, Simon and Meg, I have barely touched the surface.

Diamond Blackfan Anaemia

What is Diamond Blackfan Anaemia?

DBA is a disorder of the bone marrow, which malfunctions and fails to make enough red blood cells, which carry oxygen to the body's tissues. People with DBA carry an increased risk of several serious complications related to their malfunctioning bone marrow: certain cancers, acute myeloid leukaemia (AML) and a type of bone cancer, osteosarcoma. Approximately half of individuals with DBA have physical abnormalities. About one-third have slow growth leading to short stature. The severity of DBA varies. It is extremely rare and affects just 125 people in UK and 1,100 world-wide.

Research into the cause of DBA and other related bone marrow failures is being carried out at St Mary's Hospital Paddington. More research is urgently needed. Profits from this book will go to Diamond Blackfan Anaemia charity and to Heidi.

www.diamondblackfan.org

HEIDI

Lightning Source UK Ltd.
Milton Keynes UK
UKOW06f0731220215

246683UK00006B/13/P